The Gen X Series

ENGLISH OLYMPIAD

4

Useful for English Olympiads Conducted at School, National & International Levels

Author
Sahil Gupta

Peer Reviewer
Manasvi Vohra

Strictly According to the Latest Syllabus of English Olympiad

V&S PUBLISHERS

Published by:

V&S PUBLISHERS

F-2/16, Ansari road, Daryaganj, New Delhi-110002
☎ 23240026, 23240027 • *Fax:* 011-23240028
✉ info@vspublishers.com • ⊕ www.vspublishers.com

Online Brandstore: amazon.in/vspublishers

Regional Office : Hyderabad
5-1-707/1, Brij Bhawan (Beside Central Bank of India Lane)
Bank Street, Koti, Hyderabad - 500 095
☎ 040-24737290
✉ vspublishershyd@gmail.com

Follow us on: f   t   in

BUY OUR BOOKS FROM: | AMAZON | | FLIPKART |

© Copyright: V&S PUBLISHERS
ISBN 978-93-579407-2-6
New Edition

Publisher's Note

General Trade and Mass Appeal books across various genres have helped **V&S Publishers** to gain widespread popularity. In a short span of 10 years, we have successfully published more than 1000 titles across 9 languages in our 50 subject categories. Being into the publishing business for about 40 years, we have always been a dynamic publishing house, with a massive distribution network, across India; including E-commerce platforms.

Understanding the need of inculcating knowledge and developing a spirit of healthy competition amongst students to make them ready for the world outside schools and colleges; we created Olympiad Series under the **GEN X SERIES Imprint** which, owning to its rich content and unique representation became popular amongst students, in no time. The motivation is not to improve marks in terms of numbers, but is to make sure that the students are already prepared to face competitive environment with respect to college admissions and cracking various entrance examinations, while ensuring their conceptual clarity.

Published for classes 1-10 across subjects English, Mathematics, Science, Computers, General Knowledge, the books are unlike any other in the market and are written in a guidebook pattern and exhaustively include examples and Multiple-Choice Questions.

Here, we present the latest Edition of **ENGLISH OLYMPIAD CLASS 4.**

Unique Features of the book are as follows:

☞ Authored by Subject Matter Experts' and Peer reviewed by School Principals and HOD's for the respective subjects

☞ Books based on principles of Applied Psychology and Bloom's Taxonomy

☞ Suited for Olympiad Examinations held at School level, National level & International Level irrespective of organizing body.

☞ The only Olympiad Book in India written in Guidebook Pattern with Concise Theory, images and illustrations.

☞ Exhaustively include Examples, MCQs, Subjective Questions, and HOTS with Answer Keys & Solutions.

☞ Multiple Model Papers for thorough practice also given inside the book with solutions.

☞ OMR sheets appended at the end of the book for simulating exam environment.

Besides, we are also planning to launch an App very soon for the Olympiad preparation which further testifies our constant endeavor to keep up with student demands. We have made sure to closely follow syllabus patterns of not only Olympiad conducting bodies but also education boards & organizations like CBSE and NCERT, to make sure that our books prove useful to students; helping them to boost their academic performance in schools as well.

P.S. While every care has been taken to ensure the correctness of the content, if you come across any error, howsoever minor, do not hesitate to discuss with teachers while pointing that out to us in no uncertain terms.

We wish you All the Best!

DISTINCTIVE

01 LEARNING OBJECTIVES

They list the whole chapter as subtopics, helping the teachers to guide children in a step-by-step manner.

02 DID YOU KNOW

Enhance your knowledge by getting acquainted with some amazing facts across various subjects like science, Mathematics and English.

03 MULTIPLE CHOICE QUESTIONS

MCQs act as an excellent learning aid, helping you to understand and work on your mistakes.

04 THINGS TO REMEMBER

A quick recap of the chapter in a summarized format helps in faster revision along with conceptual clarity.

05 HOTS

The High Order Thinking Questions aim to help the student to solve Application-based questions and gain practical understanding of the subject.

FEATURES

SUBJECTIVE QUESTIONS

Help to place the knowledge gained in orderly fashion by using "WI I" questions, mostly in the form of bullet points.

06

ACHIEVER'S SECTION

Offers a quick revision of the book along with some new facts for the students to discover.

07

A SET OF OMR SHEETS

To allow the student to practice question in an exam-like format which would help them to get the "feel" of how Olympiad exams take place.

08

MODEL TEST PAPERS

Two model test papers are provided at the end of each book, which help the student to test the knowledge which they have gained after thorough reading of all chapters.

09

ANSWER KEY & SOLUTIONS

Detailed Answer Key along with explanations aid the pupil to indentify, understand the mistakes they make during the course of Olympiad preparation.

10

COMPLEMENT SCHOOL SYLLABI

The syllabi across all Olympiad examination closely follow the pattern of academic books. Hence, they not only provide a competitive examination experience, but also help to revise topics for school examinations as well, while strengthening conceptual precision.

ENHANCEMENT OF ANALYTICAL & LOGICAL REASONING

Practicing analytical ability questions, not only helps in developing intellectual ability but also plays a vital role in building critical thinking ability which helps an individual to think about a question or a crisis like situation in day to day life; from all aspects and directions.

Note to Parents

Dear Parents,

Olympiad examinations come with a plethora of advantages. First and foremost among such advantages is the application of knowledge studied, in the form of multiple-choice questions. It helps the child not only to step away from rote learning, but also helps them to exhibit their competencies across various subjects.

In addition to this, Olympiads help the student to understand the importance of revision and practice, and to imbibe upon these practices; which also prove useful in academic performance of the child.

The Olympiads are conducted across multiple subjects, and help the child to recognize their field of interest, thereby encouraging the students to make a career in the field where they can excel the most.

However, cognitive development of a child is not just limited to the four walls of classroom. Following steps can be encouraged by you, to ensure their ward is able to grasp various concepts with ease or lesser difficulty:

☞ **Eat a balanced diet:** Ensure intake of vitamins and minerals to keep you active. Include fruits and super foods like millet in your diet to ensure healthy functioning of organs. Huge intake of junk food should be avoided.

☞ **Indulge in outdoor activities:** Outdoor games break the monotony of life. Play your heart out in greenery to keep yourself alert, active and fit.

☞ **Sleep well:** A sound sleep of 7-8 hours refreshes the brain and makes it ready to understand new topics with more clarity. A sleep derived person faces difficulty in doing even the simplest tasks of day to day life.

☞ **Reduce your Screen time:** More screen time leads to not only weakening of eyesight but decreases concentration span. Regulated Screen time should be encouraged

☞ **Do not hesitate to raise a hand:** Having a doubt in class? Do not hesitate to ask your parents or teachers. This ensures more Conceptual Clarity and hence leads to Application based understanding of various subjects and topics.

☞ **Teach and Learn:** No need to do rote-learning. Once you understand a topic teach or explain it to your friends, siblings and parents. It brings clarity and ensures the child does his revision this way.

☞ **Keep smiling:** A positive attitude promotes a growth mindset and encourages the child to be more inquisitive and try to learn something new, everyday!

HAPPY LEARNING!

Contents

SECTION 1
WORD AND
STRUCTURE KNOWLEDGE

Spellings and Collocation

1

CHAPTER SUMMARY

Spellings are defined as the formation of meaningful words from letters of the Alphabet. Here are some common rules to keep in mind when you are learning how to spell English words. There are exceptions to almost all of these rules but these are valid in most cases.

1. Generally, if you add a prefix to a word, it does not change the original and correct spelling. Examples: un + sure = unsure

   un + interested = uninterested

2. The letter I always appears before the alphabet E, except when these appear after C. As a basic rule this is great, but it fails to define words like ancient, leisure, neighbour. However, there are a number of other rules that you can use to help decode the spelling of an unfamiliar word. Examples: believe, field, relief etc.

i before e...
except when you
run a feisty heist on
a weird beige foreign
neighbour.

3. The letter Q is always followed by U. In this case, the U is not considered to be a vowel. Examples: queue, cheque, plaque etc.

4. The letter S never follows X. For example, even when words which end in X form their plurals, they never form plurals simply by adding S. Examples: fox is foxes, for box is boxes.

5. When we have to change or add words which begin with a vowel to words which end with E which is not pronounced, we delete the final E. Examples: come becomes coming and hope becomes hoping.

> **TRIVIA**
>
> English is recognized as an official language in a total of 67 different countries, as well as 27 non-sovereign entities.

6. When we are adding to a word that ends with the letter Y, then the Y changes to the letter I if it is preceded by a consonant.

   Example: the word apply will change to applied;

7. Another common rule in the English language is about the word All when it is changed or added to other words. When written alone, the correct spelling of all has two L's but when used as a prefix,

we use only one L. Example: also and almost.

8. As a rule, words which end in a vowel and Y can add the suffix -ed or -ing without making any other change. Example: buy + ing = buying

A collocation is a sequence of words which are usually used together.

You can look at these words as always being together. They are like best friends.

A good example with which all of us are familiar is 'fast food.' We all know that the food is not fast, it is just served fast. Also, no another synonym of 'fast' conveys the same meaning – you don't say 'quick food' or 'speed food.'

It is a good idea to learn collocations because then you can use a language more naturally and like a native.

Let's try to understand how collocations work.

Noun Collocations

(a) **Noun + Noun:** These are phrases which have two nouns jumbled together. Like a 'round of golf,' 'bar of soap,' 'crown of thorns,', 'piece of chalk' among many many others. Collective nouns fall in this category. Like a pride of lions.

(b) **Noun + Verb:** These are phrases which are made up of a noun and a verb. Like a 'dog's bark', 'lion's roar'

You understand how the collocations work. See more examples of collocations below.

Verb collocations

(a) **Verb + Noun:** 'Jump a red light,' 'go haywire,' 'give a presentation,' etc.

(b) **Verb + Adverb:** 'Pray fervently,' 'shout madly,' 'dance joyfully' etc.

Adjective collocations

(a) **Adjective + Noun:** 'Greener pastures,' 'mild headache,' 'disciplined child'

(b) **Adverb + Adjective:** 'completely satisfied,' 'utterly stupid,' 'fully functional' etc.

MUST REMEMBER

➡ The letter I always appears before the alphabet E, except when these appear after C.

➡ When we have to change or add words which begin with a vowel to words which end with E which is not pronounced, we delete the final E.

PRACTICE EXERCISE

I. Pick the correct option for the following sentences

1. My uncle is a priest/preist.
2. The name of the qween/queen of England is Elizabeth.
3. I have just one box here, the rest of the boxes are in the other room.
4. We should give your mother the correct information. She should not be misinformed/misenformed.
5. Do you want to drive? Sure, I like driving/driveing.
6. It nearly midnight. Allmost/almost your birthday.
7. There was a robbery in the club last night. The theif/thief took all the electronics.
8. Can you supply the food tomorrow? Can you have it supplied/supplyed by 4:00 pm.
9. Do you want to play TT? No thanks, I played/plaid this morning.
10. I am aware of the class time table. I am unaware/unawair of the date of the exam.
11. Also/allso bring me a glass of water.
12. Please write the report. Writing/writeing it is very important.
13. Eat your breakfast quickly/kwickly.
14. Wash those fruits, you should never eat them unwashed/unvashed.
15. I will get my breifcase/briefcase.
16. Where did Naina stay during her vacation? She stayed/staid at the Meriton hotel.
17. Multiply 2 by 3. 2 multiplyed/multiplied by 3 is 6.
18. Give your sister the clothes. I am giveing/giving them to her.
19. I am almost/allmost finished with the project.
20. I can help carry some of the bags. Thanks, I had carried/carryed most of them yesterday.
21. Fox is a dangerous animal. Foxes/foxs live in the forest.
22. Do you want a peice/piece of the cake?
23. Please keep the voice low. Keeping/keepeeng it low is important.
24. Are you sure? I am actually unsuere/unsure.
25. I will type the document. It is already typed/typped.
26. Ducks qwack/quack.
27. Is the linen washed or unvashed/unwashed?
28. Green tea relaxes/relaxs me.
29. My niece/neice is twelve years old.
30. Vivek will allso/also be joining us for lunch.

II. Choose the correct option from the given choices to complete the sentences.

> Waste Rich Litter Spirit Warm Works Falling Permission Making Strong Heavy Record Red handed Wish Fluent Bitterly Threw Take Feel Maintenance

1. I have been working for too long. I think I will _____ a break.
2. Mukul was outside, _____ a phone call when they were looking for him inside the hall.
3. Don't _____time. It will be evening before you know it.
4. She cried _____when she heard that India had lost the match.
5. It was December and the snow was _____.
6. My friend has just adopted a _____ of puppies.
7. There are so many institutes which promise to teach people _____English.
8. Delhi has a very _____ history.

9. Richa is late because she is stuck in _____ traffic.

10. Rahul does not drink milk. He only likes _____ coffee.

11. Everyone likes Anna, she is a very _____ hearted person.

12. Ahmad scored the highest runs ever in the county. He broke the _____.

13. I am not surprised Zian came first. He _____ hard.

14. Suhail took the teacher's _____ before he left class.

15. It was Bhawna's 22nd birthday. Her father _____a party for her.

16. Please don't be shy. _____free to take more if you want.

17. Bhuvan was caught _____. He will have to suffer punishment.

18. They stood by each other. This is called team _____.

19. Cut the cake and make a _____.

20. He spends about thirty thousand rupees on clothes every month. He is very high _____.

II. Pick the correct option to form the correct sentence.

1. Let's order from this place. It has no-charge/free delivery in this area.

2. Delhi is experiencing extremely high heat/temperatures this summer.

3. You should definitely buy this car. It is value for money/finances.

4. Don't waste any more energy on this. It is a lost/forgotten cause.

5. Don't delay the work too much. Time walks very fast/flies!

6. When Sachin saw his new bike, he started dancing with joy/fear.

7. This is not difficult for mom, this is a piece of food/cake.

8. You can see a lion in the zoo but you can't hear the lion's shout/roar.

9. Please lower the volume, I have a stout/mild headache.

10. She does not understand anything. She is utterly stupid/fool.

HOTS

I. Form the correct questions for the following answers:

1. Yes, I love Marathi food.

2. My roll number is 38.

3. No, I will not be able to pick the things up today.

4. I call granny every day.

5. No, It is not safe to drive at night on a highway.

II. Fill in the blank with the correct options given in the box.

| In Each At By On You Across |
| Their At In On By |

1. The ring is kept safely _____the box.

2. His match was _____ the 13th.

3. She was _____ the bank when Anil called.

4. The books can be bought at that shop _____ the road.

5. The birds come out _____spring.

6. There is no dust _____ the rack. I cleaned everything.

7. Are you leaving _____train or _____ car?

8. The train will pass _____ Kolkata.

9. We always eat _____this restaurant.

10. Are _____feeling cold?

Animals, Housing and Food

2

> **Learning Objectives :** In this chapter, students will learn about:
> ✓ Animals and their types
> ✓ Household items
> ✓ Different types of clothing

CHAPTER SUMMARY

The natural habitat of different animals can be at different places. They can be found in the forest in between the greenery, on the hills, the desert. Let's begin by looking at the some of the places where you will find animals in the wild.

1. **Forest:** Here are the animals that live in the wild.
   (a) Tigers
   (b) Lions
   (c) Pythons
   (d) Wolves
   (e) Foxes
   (h) Elephants
   (j) Monkeys
   (h) Bison
   (i) Antelopes
   (j) Rhinoceros
   (k) Crocodiles
   (l) Giraffes

2. **Desert:** You must have heard a lot about these animals which are found in the Indian desert. The camel, in fact is most commonly associated with the desert.

   (a) Lizards
   (b) Snakes
   (c) Eagles
   (d) Sand cats
   (e) Fennec Fox
   (f) Camels

3. **Cities:** A lot of animals live freely and on their own even in the cities. These animals are not all pets but live in and around the cities.
   (a) Pigeons
   (b) Squirrels
   (c) Racoons
   (d) Dogs
   (e) Goats
   (f) Cows
   (g) Crones

Humans and animals live in harmony in a lot of places. When animals are domesticated and learn to live around humans, they are called pets. Let us look at some of the common pets.

1. **Domestic pets:**
   (a) Dogs
   (b) Cats
   (c) Goldfish
   (d) Ducks
   (e) Turtles
   (f) Sheep
   (g) Pigs

(h) Horse
(i) Parrots
(j) Guinea-pig
(k) Rabbit

2. **Farms:**
   (a) **Horse:** The horse has been used for centuries for going from one place to another and for a lot of other farm work.
   (b) **Cows:** These are found on farms because of the milk that they give and for tilling the farm land.
   (c) **Chicken:** They are bred for eggs.
   (d) **Ducks:** These make for great farm animals and are kept for their eggs.
   e. **Geese:** Geese are just like ducks, also raised for eggs.
   f. **Dogs:** These are used for security, for hunting and other purposes.
   g. **Sheep:** Utility as well as wool come from these animals.
   h. **Buffalo:** Milk and hard work are all part of the buffalo's work at farm.

3. **Zoo:** These are animals, who are only partly domesticated, however many of them are wild animals. They live in the open but are not completely free.
   (a) Tigers
   (b) Elephants
   (c) Deer
   (d) Peacocks
   (e) Buffalo
   (f) Black buck
   (g) Giraffe
   (h) Zebras
   (i) Hog-deer
   (j) Rhinoceros
   (k) Crocodiles
   (l) Monkeys
   (m) Lions

Household Things

Let us look at household things according to their place in the house.

1. **Drawing room/Living room:** The things you find in a drawing room include:

(a) Sofa set
(b) Centre table
(c) Flower vase
(d) Carpet
(e) Side table
(f) T.V.
(g) Music system and speakers
(h) Paintings and other decorative things like statues, all hangings etc.

2. **Kitchen:** The things you find in a kitchen include:
   (a) Stove
   (b) Utensils like pots, pans, plates, bowls, storage boxes etc.
   (c) Vegetables like onions, potatoes etc.
   (d) Fridge – to store food which might otherwise go bad.
   (e) Microwave oven
   (f) Dining table
   (g) Cutlery like spoons, forks, plates etc.
   (h) Spices like salt, turmeric, pepper, nutmeg, cinnamon, cardamom, cloves etc.
   (i) Chimney

3. **Study room:** The things you find in a study room include:
   (a) Study table
   (b) Chair
   (c) Books and note books
   (d) Bags
   (e) Bookshelves
   (f) Stationery like pens, pencils, erasers, staplers, calendars, sharpeners etc.
   (g) Computer
   (h) Study lamp
   (i) Filing cabinet

4. **Bedroom:** The things you find in a bedroom include:
   (a) Bed
   (b) Side-stool
   (c) Cupboards
   (d) Clothes like shirts, pants, frocks, socks, handkerchiefs, ties, scarves, gloves, coats etc.

(e) Mirror

(f) Cosmetics like powder, lipsticks, creams, lotions, gels, nail paints etc.

(g) Table lamp

5. **Bathroom:** The things you find in a bathroom include:

   (a) Toiletries like soap, shampoo, razor, shaving cream, lotions, tooth brush, tooth paste etc.

   (b) Mirror

   (c) Towels

   (d) Bathroom scales

   (e) Room freshener

   (f) Buckets, mugs, shower, shower curtain

6. **Laundry room:** The things you find in a laundry room include:

   (a) Washing machine

   (b) Dryer

   (c) Soap, fabric softener etc,

   (d) Clothes basket

   (e) Ironing table

7. **Terrace:** The things that you find on the terrace include:

   (a) Plants

   (b) Benches

8. **Garage:** The things that you find in a garage include:

   (a) Vehicles like car, motorcycle

   (b) Cycles

   (c) Old clothes, Toys etc.

   (d) Gardening tools

   (e) Old/extra furniture

9. **Prayer room:** The things that you find in a prayer room include:

   (a) Idols of god

   (b) Incense sticks

   (c) Carpet or stools to sit on and pray

   (d) Lamps or candles

   (e) Flowers

   (f) Prayer books

10. **Gym:** The things that you find in a gym include:

    (a) Exercise mat

(b) Music system

(c) Exercising machines

(d) Mirror

(e) Changing room/curtain

(f) Water dispenser

(g) Coat/clothes hanger

Food

In modern times, like everything else, food also has to go through machines before it comes to us. We have machines for everything, for sowing the grains, for reaping, processing and packaging them, to actually cooking the food and packaging it. Let us take a look at some of the common ways in which we find food today.

Natural food

This refers to the foods which have not been processed with machines before they are consumed.

Fruits

Fruits are mostly eaten in the form in which they appear in nature. Even though chemicals are now used frequently in the farming of fruits, since we consume them in their natural form, we consider them a very good kind of natural food. Some examples:

1. Bananas
2. Mangoes
3. Strawberries
4. Melons
5. Grapes
6. Oranges
7. Kiwis

Vegetables

Vegetables are slightly different from fruits in that they are usually eaten after being cooked. They are not usually eaten as they appear in nature. Look at the following common examples:

1. Potatoes
2. Peas
3. Cauliflower
4. Cabbage
5. Different kinds of gourds like bottle gourds, bittergourds etc.

6. Brinjal
7. Capsicum
8. Carrots
9. Lettuce
10 Turnips

Grains

Grains are the naturally grown foods that are consumed after being cooked but the processing does not drastically change the nature of the grain. The processing usually includes converting the grains into flour for ease of cooking o polishing the grain. The common grains include:

1. Wheat
2. Rice
3. Millet
4. Sorghum
5. Barley
6. Semolina
7. Rye
8. Bulgar
9. Corn
10 Oats
11. Bran
12. Couscous

Processed Food

Fruits and Vegetables

Fruits and vegetables are eaten in their natural form but they are also eaten in preserved form in tins and cans. The following fruits and vegetables are most commonly found in tins and cans:

1. Tomatoes
2. Corn
3. Peaches
4. Juices of fruits and vegetables like apple, mango, tomato, pineapple etc.
5. Jams and jellies of fruits and vegetables like strawberry, pineapple etc.
6. Pickles of vegetables like carrots, chillies, cucumber, beans, lime etc.
7. Dried fruits are also a fairly common kind of processed food.

Packaged or Cooked Food

Food items that are available in packaged form, and are ready to eat are called packaged food. This kind of food is also called junk food. The most popular kind of junk food include:

1. Burgers
2. Patties
3. Chowmein
4. Pizza
5. Chips
6. Packaged cookies
7. Ready to eat food
8. Frozen food
9. Aerated drinks
10. Ketchup
11. Cereals
12. Artificial sweeteners
13. Packaged cheese
14. Ice cream
15. Doughnuts
16. Fatty and packaged meats like sausages
17. Milkshakes
18. Candies
19. Powdered milk/ baby food

Clothes

The clothes that people wear can be classified according to the occasions on which people wear them. For example, men, women and children all wear different kinds of clothes. They also have different kinds of clothes that they wear on different occasions. Let us look at some of them.

Casual Clothes

These are the clothes which you wear most of the time. The most important aspect of this kind of clothes is comfort. Let us look at some of the clothes which fall under this category:

(a) **Men's casual clothes:**
  1. Jeans
  2. T-shirts
  3. Kurta pajama
  4. Shorts
  5. Dungarees

6. Chinos
7. Loafers
8. Slacks
9. Sweat shirt

(b) Women's casual clothes:
1. Jeans
2. T-shirts
3. Tops
4. Sweat shirts
5. Shorts
6. Bloomers
7. Summer dresses
8. Maxi
9. Jumpsuit

(c) Children's casual clothes:
1. T-shirts
2. Jeans
3. Frocks
4. Dungarees

TRIVIA

The dent between your nose and your lips is called a Philtrum.

Formal Clothes

These are the kind of clothes you wear when you go to office. Let us look at some examples:

(a) Men's formal wear:
1. Pants
2. Shirts
3. Waistcoats
4. Jackets
5. Coats
6. Formal shoes
7. Tie
8. Pocket handkerchief

(b) Women's formal wear:
1. Suits
2. Jackets
3. Trousers
4. Sarees
5. Salwar kameez
6 Formal dress

Sports wear

These are the clothes which are worn when one plays sports. These clothes are made keeping in mind activity and ease of movement.

Both men and women wear the following kinds of clothes while playing:
1. Shorts
2. T-shirts
3. Sweatshirts
4. Track suits
5. Sport shoes or for the particular sport playing like football.
6. Headbands and wristbands

MUST REMEMBER

➡ When animals are domesticated and learn to live around humans, they are called pets.
➡ Natural food refers to the foods which have not been processed with machines before they are consumed.
➡ Food items that are available in packaged form, and are ready to eat are called packaged food.

I. **What can the following items be categorised as?**

1. Sharpeners : _____
2. Plates : _____
3. Turmeric : _____
4. Socks : _____
5. Lotion : _____
6. Pans : _____
7. Salt : _____
8. Stapler : _____
9. Frock : _____
10. Nutmeg : _____
11. Gels : _____
12. Pots : _____
13. Car : _____
14. Pencils : _____
15. Vases : _____

II. **In which room of the house would you find the following?**

1. Incense sticks : _____
2. Old furniture : _____
3. Computer : _____
4. Statues : _____
5. Exercising machines : _____
6. Benches : _____
7. Towels : _____
8. T.V. : _____
9. Fridge : _____
10. Study-lamp : _____
11. Room freshener : _____
12. Prayer books : _____
13. Cycles : _____
14. Centre table : _____
15. Clothes : _____

III. **Identify what category the following kinds of foods belong to:**

1. Ketchup : _____
2. Barley : _____
3. Kiwis : _____
4. Baby food : _____
5. Apple juice : _____
6. Bulgar : _____
7. Cauliflower : _____
8. Doughnuts : _____
9. Lettuce : _____
10. Melons : _____

IV. **Which occasion do the following clothes belong to?**

1. Slacks : _____
2. Tie : _____
3. Bellies : _____
4. Frocks : _____
5. Maxi : _____
6. Formal dress : _____
7. Track suit : _____
8. Waistcoat : _____
9. Summer dresses : _____
10. Studs : _____

I. **Pick out five correct answers for all of the following places where you find animals:**

1. **Farm:** Dogs, camels, antelopes, sheep, horses, whales, cows, bison, chicken.

2. **City roads:** Wild cats, squirrels, bears, foxes, cows, tigers, dogs, pigeons, goldfish, goats.

3. **Desert:** Monkeys, wild cats, crocodiles, cames, lizards, giraffes, racoon, rabbit, eagles, guinea pigs, foxes.

4. **Zoo:** Black hog, hog-deer, rabbit, elephants, geese, horses, rhinoceros, owls, lions.

🕐🕐🕐

Emotions

Learning Objectives : In this chapter, students will learn about:
- ✓ Different emotions

CHAPTER SUMMARY

Emotions are the feelings that we experience everyday. Let us look at some of the basic emotions we go through. And how we express these emotions in words.

Let us begin with the emotion we think about the most.

Love

This is the emotion, which we share with almost everyone we like. You can use this emotions to express your love for your parents, your siblings, your friends, your teachers.

Adoration, liking, fondness, attraction, caring, tenderness, compassion, empathy etc. are feelings of love.

Joy

This is the emotion you feel whenever you are happy about something. This can be because you got a new toy or go on a vacation or eat food that you really like or you see or meet someone you love.

Delight, enjoyment, excitement, thrill, cheerfulness, pleasure, happiness, bliss, amusement, gladness, bliss etc. are feelings of joy.

Surprise

When you see or experience something that you were not expecting, you are surprised.

Amazement and astonishment feelings also similar to of surprise.

Anger

When you are going through a phase of disliking something, you experience anger.

Irritation, annoyance, agitation, frustration, rage, outrage, hate, spite, vengefulness, wrath, fury, dislike etc. are feelings of anger.

Envy

When you want something that someone else has but you don't have it and you dislike him/her because of it, you are experiencing envy.

Jealousy is another word, which is used for this emotion.

Sadness

This is the opposite of happiness.

Suffering, hurt, anguish, despair, hopelessness, gloom, unhappiness, grief, sorrow, woe, misery, melancholy, displeasure, rejection, and dejection etc. are feelings of sadness.'

Shame

This is the feeling you experience when you feel like you have done something wrong and are feeling bad about it.

Guilty, regretful, remorseful, embarrassment, humiliation are some related words.

Fear

When you are scared of something, you experience fear.

Shock, fear, horror, terror, panic, mortification, anxiety, nervousness, uneasiness, apprehension, worry, distress, dread, fright, alarm are some of the emotions directly or indirectly related to fear.

TRIVIA

Natyashastra, a Sanskrit text written by Bharata talks about 9 human emotionss: love, laughter, compassion, horrer, disgust, wonder and heroism.

MUST REMEMBER

➡ When you are scared of something, you experience fear
➡ Anger is an emotion characterized by antagonism toward someone or something you feel has deliberately done you wrong.

Place the following emotions under the correct head out of the 8 major emotions discussed in the chapter: See the example.

Jealousy : Envy

1. Caring : _____
2. Hate : _____
3. Fright : _____
4. Likeness : _____
5. Remorsefulness : _____
6. Rage : _____
7. Grief : _____
8. Astonishment : _____
9. Alarm : _____
10. Empathy : _____
11. Fury : _____
12. Gloom : _____
13. Amazement : _____
14. Guilty : _____
15. Terror : _____

HOTS

Select the correct option from the ones given for each emotion.

1. Woe
   (a) Love   (b) Envy
   (c) Sadness   (d) Shame
2. Thrill
   (a) Happiness   (b) Love
   (c) Shame   (d) Fear
3. Regretful
   (a) Surprise   (b) Envy
   (c) Fear   (d) Shame
4. Jealousy
   (a) Fear   (b) Envy
   (c) Happiness   (d) Love
5. Fright
   (a) Happiness   (b) Love
   (c) Envy   (d) Fear
6. Hate
   (a) Anger   (b) Envy
   (c) Happiness   (d) Love
7. Fondness
   (a) Surprise   (b) Anger
   (c) Love   (d) Shame
8. Amazement
   (a) Love   (b) Hate
   (c) Anger   (d) Surprise
9. Despair
   (a) Shame   (b) Sadness
   (c) Happiness   (d) Fear
10. Humiliation
    (a) Shame   (b) Anger
    (c) Surprise   (d) Fear
11. Wrath
    (a) Sadness   (b) Anger
    (c) Fear   (d) Love
12. Bliss
    (a) Fear   (b) Envy
    (c) Happiness (d) Sadness
13. Anxiety
    (a) Surprise   (b) Happiness
    (c) Fear   (d) Sadness
14. Compassion
    (a) Shame   (b) love
    (c) envy   (d) Fear
15. Embarrassment
    (a) Shame   (b) Envy
    (c) Happiness (d) Sadness

🕐🕐🕐

Synonyms and Antonyms

4

Learning Objectives : In this chapter, students will learn about:
- ✓ Some common synonyms
- ✓ Some common antonyms

CHAPTER SUMMARY

Synonyms are the words that have the same meaning or almost the same sense.

Examples:

- Beautiful : Attractive, Pretty, Lovely, Stunning
- Fair : Just, Objective, Impartial, Unbiased
- Funny : Humorous, Comical, Hilarious, Hysterical
- Happy : Content, Joyful, Mirthful, Upbeat
- Hardworking: Diligent, Determined, Industrious, Enterprising
- Honest : Honourable, Fair, Sincere, Trustworthy
- Intelligent : Smart, Bright, Brilliant, Sharp
- Introver : Shy, Bashful, Quiet, Withdrawn
- Kind : Thoughtful, Considerate, Amiable, Gracious
- Lazy : Idle, Lackadaisical, Lethargic, Indolent
- Mean : Unfriendly, Unpleasant, Bad-tempered, Difficult
- Outgoing : Friendly, Sociable, Warm, Extroverted

- Rich : Affluent, Wealthy, Well-off, Well-to-do
- Strong : Stable, Secure, Solid, Tough
- Unhappy : Sad, Depressed, Melancholy, Miserable
- Lucky : Auspicious, Fortunate
- Positive : Optimistic, Cheerful, Sanguine
- Bossy : Controlling, Tyrannical
- Baffle : Confuse, Deceive
- Hypocrisy : Duplicity, Falseness
- Pacify : Appease, Placate
- Recalcitrant : Obstinate, Stubborn
- Turbulent : Disordered, Violent
- Valid : Authorized, Legitimate
- Old : Antiquated, Ancient, Obsolete, Extinct, Past, Venerable, Aged
- True : Genuine, Reliable, Factual, Accurate, Precise, Correct, Valid, Real
- Important : Substantial, Vital, Essential, Primary, Significant, Requisite, Critical

- Weak : Frail, Anaemic, Feeble, Infirm, Languid, Sluggish, Puny, Fragile
- Loaded : Rich
- Disconsolate : Sad
- Stalwart : Strong
- Clever : Intelligent
- Cute : Beautiful
- Truthful : Honest
- Beneficent : Kind
- Convivial : Outgoing
- Virulent : Mean
- Reserved : Introverted
- Languid : Lazy
- Jocular : Funny
- Benevolent : Fair
- Assiduous : Hardworking
- Blissful : Happy

TRIVIA

No language has more synonyms than English.

Antonyms

Antonyms are the words that mean the opposite of each other. It comes from the Greek words 'anti' for opposite and 'also similar 'nym' for name. Since, the language is complex, people may at times, disagree on what words are truly opposite in meaning to other words.

Examples:
- Fat : Skinny
- Young : Old
- Happy : Sad
- Hard : Soft
- Last : First
- Foolish : Wise
- Fast : Slow
- Warm : Cool
- Wide : Narrow
- Abundant : Scarce
- Joy : Grief
- Dark : Light
- Dangerous : Safe
- Clever : Foolish
- Early : Late
- Empty : Full
- Smart : Dumb
- Risky : Safe
- Bad : Good
- Pretty : Ugly
- Best : Worst
- Simple : Challenging
- Soft : Hard
- Worried : Calm
- Sane : Crazy
- Rich : Poor
- Cool : Hot
- Wet : Dry
- Late : Early
- Ignorant : Educated
- Big : Small
- Optimistic : Pessimistic
- Excited : Bored

MUST REMEMBER

➡ Synonyms are the words that have the same meaning or almost the same sense.
➡ Antonyms are the words that mean the opposite of each other.

PRACTICE EXERCISE

I. Select the correct synonym of the word given in capital letter in each question.

1. ACCURATE
   (a) Correct   (b) Incorrect
   (c) Wrong   (d) Possible

2. ADMIRE
   (a) Praise   (b) Allow
   (c) Obey   (d) Play

3. ANNUAL
   (a) Weekly   (b) Daily
   (c) Monthly   (d) Yearly

4. BEGIN
   (a) Close   (b) Stop
   (c) Start   (d) End

5. ANGER
   (a) Happiness   (b) Pleasure
   (c) Joy   (d) Wrath

6. ASSEMBLY
   (a) House   (b) Building
   (c) Hut   (d) Gathering

7. CONVERSATION
   (a) Sing   (b) Talk
   (c) Dance   (d) Walk

8. SEARCH
   (a) Find   (b) Loose
   (c) Lost   (d) Look

9. UNITE
   (a) Divide   (b) Separate
   (c) Part   (d) Join

10. WEALTHY
    (a) Poor   (b) Hungry
    (c) Miserable   (d) Rich

11. MIDDLE
    (a) Corner   (b) Centre
    (c) End   (d) Beginning

12. ERROR
    (a) Mistake   (b) Strong
    (c) Powerful   (d) Healthy

13. FORTUNATE
    (a) Unlucky   (b) Failed
    (c) Lucky   (d) Unsuccessful

14. GENEROUS
    (a) Kind   (b) Mean
    (c) Cruel   (d) Unpleasant

15. ORDINARY
    (a) Expensive   (b) Rare
    (c) Common   (d) Unusual

16. FOOLISH
    (a) Intelligent (b) Clever
    (c) Silly   (d) Smart

17. REPLY
    (a) Answer   (b) Ask
    (c) Question   (d) Interrogate

18. FOE
    (a) Enemy   (b) Well wisher
    (c) Friend   (d) Pal

19. ODOUR
    (a) Order   (b) Smell
    (c) Colour   (d) Taste

20. STORY
    (a) Tale   (b) Write
    (c) Start   (d) Funny

II. Select the correct antonym of the word given in capital letter.

1. ACCEPT
   (a) Reject   (b) Agree
   (c) Tiny   (d) Regard

2. AGREE
   (a) Disagree   (b) Defend
   (c) Worse   (d) Tight

3. ABSENT
   (a) Lost (b) Found
   (c) Choose (d) Present

4. ANCIENT
   (a) Old (b) Very old
   (c) Early (d) Modern

5. ATTACK
   (a) Defend (b) Damage
   (c) Hurt (d) Harm

6. BOTTOM
   (a) Top (b) Base
   (c) Floor (d) Foot

7. BLUNT
   (a) Dull (b) Rounded
   (c) Honest (d) Sharp

8. EMPTY
   (a) Blank (b) Full
   (c) Bare (d) Vacant

9. COARSE
   (a) Rough (b) Uneven
   (c) Harsh (d) Fine

10. DANGEROUS
    (a) Unsafe (b) Risky
    (c) Hazardous (d) Safe

11. EXPENSIVE
    (a) Costly (b) Dear
    (c) Cheap (d) Steep

12. DEEP
    (a) Shallow (b) Open
    (c) Tall (d) Long

13. FOOLISH
    (a) Stupid (b) Silly
    (c) Idiot (d) Wise

14. TAME
    (a) Domesticated (b) Cultivated
    (c) Pet d Wild

15. VICTORY
    (a) Defeat (b) Triumph
    (c) Win (d) Success

16. LIE
    (a) Falsehood (b) Truth
    (c) Fib (d) Story

17. SPEND
    (a) Use (b) Consume
    (c) Finish (d) Save

18. MOIST
    (a) Wet (b) Dry
    (c) Damp (d) Soaked

19. BRIGHT
    (a) Light (b) Sharp
    (c) Dull (d) Tight

20. ALONE
    (a) Lonely (b) Togetherness
    (c) Single (d) Lonesome

Choose the correct synonym of the word given in CAPITAL LETTERS.

1. ANGRY
   - (a) Calm
   - (b) Tranquil
   - (c) Annoyed
   - (d) Quite
   - (e) Cool

2. FRANK
   - (a) Bold
   - (b) Good
   - (c) Bad
   - (d) Beautiful
   - (e) Ugly

3. LAZY
   - (a) Indolent
   - (b) Fall
   - (c) Right
   - (d) Trash
   - (e) Sharp

4. OVERCOME
   - (a) Prominent
   - (b) Defeat
   - (c) Bandit
   - (d) Get
   - (e) None of these

5. POLITE
   - (a) Civil
   - (b) Danger
   - (c) Endless
   - (d) Excuse
   - (e) None of these

Nouns

Learning Objectives : In this chapter, students will learn about:
✓ Nouns and their types

CHAPTER SUMMARY

The names of person, places, animals, things or abstract ideas are called nouns. A noun can tell you 'who' or 'what.'

Examples:

Barrack Obama is a former President of *America*.

Students are at *school*.

I have found a *bunch of keys*.

Kinds of Noun

1. Proper Noun
2. Common Noun
3. Collective Noun
4. Material Noun
5. Abstract Noun

Proper Noun

Proper noun is the name of a particular person, animal, place or thing. These nouns are not normally preceded by an article or other limiting modifier as any or some , nor they are usually pluralised. Proper noun always begins with a capital letter, even in the middle of the sentence.

Examples:

Swift is one of the most fuel efficient cars.

Rohan has progressed very much.

In the sentences above the underlined words are proper nouns.

Common Noun

A common noun is a word, which is commonly used to name people, places, things or ideas. They are not the names of a single person, place or thing. A common noun begins with a lowercase letter unless it is at the beginning of a sentence. It refers to each member of a whole class sharing the features connoted by the noun.

Examples:

Cars are running on the street.

The doctors and the engineers contribute a lot to the society.

The underlined words in the above sentences are examples of common nouns.

TRIVIA

"Dreamt" is the only English word that ends in the letters "mt".

Collective Noun

A collective noun is the singular word, which is used for a group of people or things.

Examples:

Our team won the match.

A large crowd gathered in

In the above sentences the underlined words are examples of collective nouns.

Material Noun

Material noun is the name of a substance which can be measured or weighed, but cannot be counted. These nouns cannot be made plural by adding 's' to them. They have only singular form. They do not take a/an or a number in front of them.

Examples:

<u>Milk</u> is sweet.

The <u>shirt</u> is made of cloth.

In the above sentences, the underlined words are examples of material noun.

Abstract Noun

An abstract noun is the name of state, quality, feeling or an idea that we can only think of or feel, but cannot touch or see. These nouns are usually used in singular form. They don't have any physical existence.

Examples:

<u>Childhood</u> is the dawn of life.

<u>Adventure</u> is the virtue of courageous people.

In the above sentences, the underlined words are examples of abstract nouns.

MUST REMEMBER

➡ The names of person, places, animals, things or abstract ideas are called nouns.

➡ Proper noun is the name of a particular person, animal, place or thing.

➡ A common noun is a word, which is commonly used to name people, places, things or ideas.

➡ A collective noun is the singular word, which is used for a group of people or things.

➡ Material noun is the name of a substance which can be measured or weighed, but cannot be counted.

➡ An abstract noun is the name of state, quality, feeling or an idea that we can only think of or feel, but cannot touch or see.

I. **Find out the kind of noun the underlined word has from the given options.**

1. She had <u>pain</u> in her legs.
   (a) Abstract noun
   (b) Common noun
   (c) Collective noun
   (d) Material noun

2. Most of the <u>doctors</u> in our country avoid serving in rural areas.
   (a) Proper noun
   (b) Collective noun
   (c) Common noun
   (d) Material noun

3. Elephants more often move in <u>herd</u>.
   (a) Proper noun
   (b) Common noun
   (c) Material noun
   (d) Collective noun

4. <u>Students</u> sit together in the class.
   (a) Collective noun
   (b) Common noun
   (c) Proper noun
   (d) Material noun

5. <u>New York</u> is a beautiful city.
   (a) Collective noun
   (b) Common noun
   (c) Proper noun
   (d) Material noun

6. The man is known for his <u>wisdom</u>.
   (a) Proper noun
   (b) Collective noun
   (c) Material noun
   (d) Abstract noun

7. The commercial capital of India is <u>Mumbai</u>.
   (a) Common noun
   (b) Collective noun
   (c) Proper noun
   (d) Material noun

8. A <u>pair</u> of shoes
   (a) Proper noun

   (b) Common noun
   (c) Collective noun
   (d) Material noun

9. A <u>team</u> of players
   (a) Proper noun
   (b) Common noun
   (c) Material noun
   (d) Collective noun

10. The <u>length</u> of this room is four metres.
    (a) Abstract noun
    (b) Collective noun
    (c) Proper noun
    (d) Material noun

11. <u>Ram</u> is going to the market.
    (a) Proper noun
    (b) Common noun
    (c) Collective noun
    (d) Abstract noun

12. Sita went to the garden and studied a <u>flock of birds</u>.
    (a) Proper noun
    (b) Common noun
    (c) Collective noun
    (d) Abstract noun

13. The women went to see the <u>butterflies</u>.
    (a) Proper noun
    (b) Common noun
    (c) Collective noun
    (d) Abstract noun

14. Thomas Edison invented the <u>light bulb</u>.
    (a) Proper noun
    (b) Common noun
    (c) Collective noun
    (d) Abstract noun

15. <u>Birbal</u> was Emperor Akbar's favourite minister.
    (a) Proper noun
    (b) Common noun
    (c) Collective noun
    (d) Abstract noun

16. Dr. Rajendra Prasad was the first President of India.
    (a) Proper noun   (b) Common noun
    (c) Collective noun   (d) Abstract noun

17. The soldier was awarded for his bravery.
    (a) Proper noun   (b) Common noun
    (c) Collective noun   (d) Abstract noun

18. We have a large herd of cows, which are brought in for milking every day.
    (a) Proper noun   (b) Common noun
    (c) Collective noun   (d) Abstract noun

19. One should always tell the truth.
    (a) Proper noun
    (b) Common noun
    (c) Collective noun
    (d) Abstract noun

20. Charity begins at home.
    (a) Proper noun
    (b) Common noun
    (c) Collective noun
    (d) Abstract noun

HOTS

Fill in the blanks with appropriate noun:

1. There was no _____ among the rotten apples.
   (a) kind   (b) beauty
   (c) fresh   (d) choice

2. There is a cut throat _____ in every trade.
   (a) market   (b) choice
   (c) competition (d) familiarity

3. A ____ of people gathered at the meeting.
   (a) flight   (b) herd
   (c) crowd   (d) swarm

4. The farmer took his _____ of cattle for grazing.
   (a) bunch   (b) mob
   (c) army   (d) herd

5. The Himalayas are the highest _____ snow covered mountains in the world.
   (a) volley   (b) chain
   (c) row   (d) shoal

Pronouns

6

> **Learning Objectives :** In this chapter, students will learn about:
> ✓ Pronouns and their types

CHAPTER SUMMARY

A pronoun is a word that stand in place of a noun or a noun phrase in their absence. Its meaning depends on the noun to which it refers. Usually this noun, which the pronoun replaces, occurs in the previous sentence.

Example:

Rishabh is a good student. <u>He</u> always scores well.

Here, <u>He</u> stands for Rishabh who has been mentioned in the previous sentence.

There are different kinds of pronouns:

Personal pronoun

The example you read above is of a personal pronoun. These are pronouns which stand in the place of people. I, we, you, she, he, they are all personal pronouns. These can be used in the first person (I, me, mine, we), second person (you, your) or third person (she, he, they, their, them, it).

Example:

<u>I</u> go to the temple every Tuesday.

Demonstrative pronouns

These stand in the place of a specific animal, thing or person. These include words like this, these, those, them, that etc. They demonstrate a specific thing or a person. Examples:

<u>That</u> is my favourite chocolate.

<u>Those</u> are his shoes.

<u>These</u> are silly mistakes.

Did you buy <u>these</u> bags?

Reflexive pronouns and emphatic

These are used when a person or an object performs an action on itself. This means that they refer back to the subject within the same sentence. The easiest way to identify these is through the '-self' suffix after the personal pronouns like my, it, them etc.

Examples:

Saurabh kicked <u>himself</u> for getting a wrong question in the exam.

I cleaned my car <u>myself</u>.

If you want more tea, please help <u>yourself</u>.

In the first sentence, 'yourself' refers to you in the first phrase. In the second sentence, you does not refer to 'I' and so it cannot be called a reflexive pronoun. In the second sentence, yourself is used to put emphasis on 'you' and hence it is called 'Emphatic pronoun.'

Reciprocal pronouns and Distributive pronouns

These are used when there is more than one subject and the sentence requires you to refer to the mutual relationship between the two (or more subject). These include phrases like each other, one another etc.

Examples:

We should live in peace with <u>one another</u>.

Look at the following two sentences:

Both the sisters stood in front of the mirror and looked at <u>themselves</u>.

Both the sisters stood in front of the mirror and looked at <u>each other</u>.

In the first sentence, themselves is a reflexive noun and that is why it means that each sister standing in front of the mirror is looking at only herself and not the other.

In the second sentence, each sister is looking at the other. That is why it is reciprocal.

When 'each' is used to refer to a single 'general' person like:

Each of the contestants won a gift voucher.

This is called a distributive pronoun. This pronoun talks about persons or things one at a time. Examples of this pronoun include; each, either and neither.

Possessive pronouns

As the name suggests, these are used when one wants to indicate possession. These include words like mine, hers, ours, yours etc. This pronoun tells you that an object belongs to a person or a group.

Example:

She wanted to buy *their* gift as soon as possible.

Indefinite pronouns

These are used when one wants to refer to a non-specific person or a group of people. It can also be used to refer to people in negation like nobody. These include words like anyone, everyone, someone, somebody etc. Since they don't talk about a person in particular (for that we use the demonstrative pronoun) they are known as indefinite pronouns.

Example:

Everyone should follow traffic rules.

Interrogative pronoun

These are used when you wish to ask which person performed a particular action. These include words like who, whom, which etc.

Example:

Who removed the jar of water from the table?

Relative pronouns

These are used when you refer to a noun which has already been mentioned in the sentence. These include words like who, which, that, those etc. Relative pronouns join two sentences which describe two 'actions' performed by/on the same subject.

Example:

This is the pencil which my mother bought for me.

Here, the two actions are: This is 'the pencil' and my mother bought 'this pencil' for me. 'Which' is the pronoun which joins/forms the relationship between the two actions. To know when a pronoun is an interrogative pronoun and when it is a relative pronoun, remember that a relative pronoun always comes after the noun to which it refers. If it is referring to another noun/subject, it is an interrogative pronoun. Consider the following question:

I asked who the man in brown was?

Here 'who' refers to the man in brown and not I.

MUST REMEMBER

- A pronoun is a word that stand in place of a noun or a noun phrase in their absence.
- Reflexive pronouns and emphatic are used when a person or an object performs an action on itself.
- Reciprocal pronouns and Distributive pronouns are used when there is more than one subject and the sentence requires you to refer to the mutual relationship between the two.

PRACTICE EXERCISE

I. **Use the correct form of pronoun to complete the following sentences:**

1. _____ is a pronoun? It is a word which is used in the place of a noun. (interrogative)
   (a) Who   (b) It
   (c) Them   (d) What

2. Priya wants to paint _____room pink. (possessive)
   (a) Them   (b) Herself
   (c) Her   (d) Who

3. _____ people come here to shop even in early morning. (Indefinite)
   (a) Her   (b) Some
   (c) Any   (d) Everybody

4. _____ can still go to the playground, it's just 7pm. (Personal)
   (a) Each
   (b) Anybody
   (c) It
   (d) You

5. _____of the trains will do. I just need to get to Srinagar. (Distributive)
   (a) Any   (b) Himself
   (c) Each other   (d) Those

6. I like those clothes _____ have pockets. (relative)
   (a) Themselves   (b) I
   (c) Who   (d) Which

7. Saumya has hurt _____. (Reflexive)
   (a) Herself   (b) It
   (c) Which   (d) That

8. This book is _____. I bought it in Shimla. (possessive)
   (a) It   (b) Mine
   (c) His   (d) They

9. This is the house _____ I was talking about. (Relative)
   (a) Itself   (b) Who
   (c) Whose   (d) Which

10. Don't worry so much this time _____ will definitely be selected for the team. (Personal)
    (a) You   (b) Who
    (c) Which   (d) That

11. _____ has called back from the shop. I am still waiting. (Indefinite)
    (a) Few   (b) Nobody
    (c) Itself   (d) Which

12. Is _____the movie you were talking about? (Demonstrative)
    (a) Which   (b) They
    (c) That   (d) My

13. _____ must be careful while one is crossing the road. (indefinite)
    (a) Myself   (b) One
    (c) It   (d) I

14. I will _____ lock up the shop. (emphatic)
    (a) Itself   (b) Themselves
    (c) Myself   (d) Yourself

15. _____ knows the correct answer? (interrogative)
    (a) Who   (b) I
    (c) That   (d) Which

II. **Choose what kind of pronoun the word given in italics:**

1. *This* is the book that I was looking for.
   (a) Interrogative   (b) Relative
   (c) Reflexive   (d) Demonstrative

2. *That* is the car I was talking about.
   (a) Personal   (b) Interrogative
   (c) Reflexive   (d) Demonstrative

3. The boy *who* broke my car window is Mr. Bisht's son.
   (a) Relative   (b) Personal
   (c) Emphatic   (d) Reflexive

4. *Everyone* has a hobby.
   (a) Distributive   (b) Relative
   (c) Indefinite   (d) Personal

5. The prime minister *himself* congratulated her.
    (a) Relative (b) Reflexive
    (c) Personal (d) Emphatic

6. What is *that* stain because of!
    (a) Demonstrative (b) Personal
    (c) Indefinite (d) Relative

7. *Each* student will get to see the programme.
    (a) Demonstrative (b) Personal
    (c) Distributive (d) Indefinite

8. The cat went into the room and slept on *its* cushion.
    (a) Personal (b) Possessive
    (c) Indefinite (d) Reflexive

9. Rita is my cousin *who* lives in New York.
    (a) Relative (b) Personal
    (c) Indefinite (d) Reflexive

10. *You* are a good dancer.
    (a) Interrogative (b) Personal
    (c) Possessive (d) Indefinite

11. *Who* is knocking? Please open the door and see.
    (a) Indefinite (b) Possessive
    (c) Reflexive (d) Interrogative

12. The two friends looked at *each other* and laughed.
    (a) Reciprocal (b) Possessive
    (c) Reflexive (d) Indefinite

13. The athlete *who* won the Olympic medal lives in this street.
    (a) Indefinite (b) Relative
    (c) Reflexive (d) possessive

14. Rohit looked at *his* watch and sighed.
    (a) Interrogative (b) Indefinite
    (c) Possessive (d) Reflexive

15. *Each* city has its own pace.
    (a) Indefinite
    (b) Distributive
    (c) Possessive
    (d) Interrogative

HOTS

Choose the pronoun in each statement and choose under whichvariety does it fall into.

1. I thought you knew him.
    (a) Demonstrative (b) Personal
    (c) Possessive (d) Reflexive

2. These books are ours.
    (a) Demonstrative (b) Personal
    (c) Possessive (d) Reflexive

3. We explained how it worked for us.
    (a) Demonstrative (b) Personal
    (c) Possessive (d) Reflexive

4. That building is theirs.
    (a) Demonstrative (b) Personal
    (c) Possessive (d) Reflexive

5. I fell down and hurt myself.
    (a) Demonstrative (b) Personal
    (c) Possessive (d) Reflexive

🕐🕐🕐

Verbs

Learning Objectives : In this chapter, students will learn about:
- ✓ Verbs and their different types

CHAPTER SUMMARY

Verbs are action words or words which describe an action. Regular and irregular verbs are the type of verbs. As the name suggests irregular verbs are those verbs which are different. They are different from other verbs in the way they form their past tense and past participle. To form the past tense and past participle of regular verbs, you only have to add the suffix '-ed.' See the following examples:

Paint + ed = painted

Clean + ed = cleaned

Irregular verbs, however, form their past tense and past participle in a different way and do not follow a single rule for the same. There is no other way of knowing the past tense of these apart from memorizing them.

There are three kinds of irregular verbs:

1. Verbs in which all the three forms of the verb, i.e the base form, the past tense and the past participle are the same. For example, all the three forms of the verb put are the same.

2. Verbs for which two of the three forms are the same. For example, both the past tense and the past participle of the verb 'catch' is 'caught'. Similar is the verb buy with the past tense and past participle being bought.

3. Verbs for which all the three forms are different. One of the most common example of this kind of verbs is 'eat'. The past tense of eat is ate and its past participle is eaten.

TRIVIA

The word "ultimate" is the last thing to happen, "penultimate" is next-to-last and "antepenultimate" is the last but two in a series; the third last.

Forms of irregular verbs
All the three forms are similar:

Base form	Past tense	Past participle
Shut	Shut	Shut
Let	Let	Let
Cut	Cut	Cut
Cost	Cost	Cost
Read	Read	Read
Hit	Hit	Hit
Hurt	Hurt	Hurt
Split	Split	Split

Only two of the three forms are the similar:

Base form	Past tense	Past participle
Catch	Caught	Caught
Bring	Brought	Brought
Fight	Fought	Fought
Think	Thought	Thought
Breed	Bred	Bred
Become	Became	Become
Build	Built	Built
Deal	Dealt	Dealt
Hang	Hung	Hung
Get	Got	Got
Lead	Led	Led
Leave	Left	Left
Speed	Sped	Sped
Meet	Met	Met
Sit	Sat	Sat
Spend	Spent	Spent
Swing	Swung	Swung
Understand	Understood	Understood
Find	Found	Found
Come	Came	Come
Dig	Dug	Dug
Hear	Heard	Heard
Hold	Held	Held
Make	Made	Made

Lend	Lent	Lent
Win	Won	Won

All the three forms are different:

Base form	Past tense	Past participle
Be	Was/were	Been
See	Saw	Seen
Forget	Forgot	Forgotten
Sing	Sang	Sung
Choose	Chose	Chosen
Eat	Ate	Eaten
Fly	Flew	Flown
Forbid	Forbade	Forbidden
Go	Went	Gone
Ring	Rang	Rung
Shrink	Shrank	Shrunk
Throw	Threw	Thrown
Tear	Tore	Torn
Take	Took	Taken
Know	Knew	Known
Write	Wrote	Written
Draw	Drew	Drawn
Show	Showed	Shown
Lie	Lay	Lain
Give	Gave	Given

MUST REMEMBER

➡ Verbs are action words or words which describe an action.

I. Rewrite each of the sentences using the correct form of the irregular verb

1. I went to the concert, she sing very well. (past participle)

   Answer: _____

2. The guitar I bought last week cost me rupees 4000. (past tense)

   Answer: _____

3. Who win the tennis match last evening? (past tense)

   Answer: _____

4. Have you see my phone? I can't find it. (past participle)

   Answer: _____

5. The bird fly over us before settling down on a tree branch. (past tense)

   Answer: _____

6. Dad become angry when he heard that we had left the TV on all night. (past tense)

   Answer: _____

7. Have you cut the cake already? We are reaching in ten minutes! (past participle)

   Answer: _____

8. When was this email write? Check the time. (past participle)

   Answer: _____

9. When was the Qutub Minar build? (past tense)

   Answer: _____

10. From all the boys in the team, Aditya was choose to represent the school. (past participle)

    Answer: _____

11. I give the chocolates to Nikhil as soon as I see him. (past tense, past tense)

    Answer: _____

12. We spend the whole evening eating pop corn and chocolates. (post tense)

    Answer: _____

13. I told her the whole incident in detail and I think she understand. (past tense)

    Answer: _____

14. Who took my watch from the table? It was take by Anand. (past participle)

    Answer: _____

15. I was telling her the movie's story but she already know it all. (past tense)

    Answer: _____

II. Choose the correct option to complete the sentence

1. Sumit showed/shown me the birthday pictures.

2. Have you ate/eaten your dinner?

3. My new tee shirt has shrunk/shrank after washing.

4. There were strawberry ice cream and chocolate ice cream. I chosen/chose chocolate.

5. By the time we reached the house, the maid was go/gone.

6. It's a beautiful guitar and it costeds/costs only 3000 rupees.

7. I meets/met Richa at Mayank's birthday party.

8. I heard/hear them practicing all of last evening.

9. The ticket was tear/torn but the ticket-checker let us in.

10. The batsman was catch/caught behind the wickets and Australia lost the match.

11. She threw/throw the water in the drain last night.

12. Naina showed/shown us her new watch. It was fabulous.

13. As soon as we entered Amit's room we saw that he had drew/drawn all over the walls.

14. Like every year, Masoom's mother had made/make Halwa on her birthday.

15. She come/came into the room and realised that there was no place to sit.

HOTS

Complete the following sentences using the correct form of the irregular verb:

1. He _____2 hours just to get the tickets.
   (a) Spends   (b) Spent
   (c) Spend   (d) Spending

2. Shweta _____ a new purse last week.
   (a) Get   (b) Getting
   (c) Gets   (d) Got

3. We last _____at Shalu's birthday party.
   (a) Met   (b) Meet
   (c) Meeting   (d) Mets

4. By the time we reached the mall, everyone was already _____
   (a) See   (b) Go
   (c) Gone   (d) Going

5. I already _____when Natasha was coming but, I still called to confirm.
   (a) Knowing   (b) Knew
   (c) Know   (d) Knows

6. Arvind _____me his number in case, there was an emergency.
   (a) Giving   (b) Gives
   (c) Gave   (d) Give

7. He _____drive a car very well. I have seen it myself.
   (a) Will   (b) Can
   (c) Could   (d) Should

8. Tomorrow Pip _____come to see Andrews. I have the confirmation.
   (a) Should
   (b) Will
   (c) Could
   (d) Can

9. It _____rain tomorrow. The sky is looking a bit grey.
   (a) Might   (b) Would
   (c) Can   (d) Could

10. _____ I see your bag please?
    (a) Would   (b) Can
    (c) Could   (d) May

⏰⏰⏰

Modals

Learning Objectives : In this chapter, students will learn about:
- ✓ Modal Verbs

CHAPTER SUMMARY

Modals are a different kind of verb. They are irregular verbs which do not behave like ordinary verbs. They are also considered to be a part of the group of verbs called 'auxiliary.'

Modals are verbs like can, could, will, would, shall, should, might, may must and ought which are used before regular verbs. When Modals are used along with ordinary verbs, they are used to express permission, possibility, potential or certainty. Other important properties of the Modals are:

1. They do not take the –s form in the third person.

   Examples:

   She can cook very well. If the modal 'can' would not have been there, the sentence would have been, She cooks well.

2. They do not have any –ing form

   Examples:

   Shweta will sing at the function. If the modal 'will' were not used, the sentence would have been, Shweta is singing at the function.

3. They do not have the infinitive form.

   The infinitive can be recognized by the 'to' which is almost always used before the verb to form the infinitive.

   Examples:

   To eat is all what Sumit cares about.

If we have to use a modal: 'To can eat is all Sumit cares about' is wrong.

TRIVIA

The ZIP in Zipcode means "Zoning Improvement Plan".

Modals which express potential or ability

1. **Can** expresses ability or potential. If you say, he can ride a bike. Then you mean to say that he has the ability to ride a bike.

2. **Could** is the past tense of 'can' and a slightly less possible version of can.

3. **May** is used to express three things; possibility in the future, to wish someone/something, to ask permission. Look at the following examples:

   (a) Possibility: I may need your help.

   (b) Wish: May you have a great year ahead!

   (c) Permission: May I come in?

4. **Might** is the past tense of 'may,' as a way of showing disapproval as well as a less possible or positive version of may. Look at the following examples:

   (a) Past tense of may: He asked if he might come in.

(b) Disapproval: You might want to check your bag before claiming your phone is missing.

(c) Less positive version of may: It might rain tomorrow.

Modals that express command, duty, advice, habit and future tense

1. **Will** is used to form the future tense and habits. Look at the following examples:

   (a) Certain future: Tomorrow will be a good day.

   (b) Habits: Amit will talk about nothing but cricket. (though this way of using 'will' is not common anymore)

2. **Would** is used as the past tense of 'will' and as a polite question. See the following examples:

   (a) She would have come but it rained.

   (b) Would you like some more sugar in your tea?

3. **Shall** is used to politely ask the advice of someone and to command someone to do/not do something. Note the examples below:

   (a) Polite advice: Shall I get this ring? (do you think I should buy this ring?)

   (b) Command: You shall not talk to your mother in this way

4. **Should** is used to talk about duty, possibility, past tense of shall. See the examples below:

   (a) Duty: You should only walk on the zebra crossing.

   (b) Possibility: She should be at the dance rehearsal.

MUST REMEMBER

➡ Modals are irregular verbs which do not behave like ordinary verbs.

PRACTICE EXERCISE

I. Choose the correct answer from the given options:

1. We will/would go to the mall tomorrow.

2. Kanika shall/should take the school's warning seriously.

3. Would/will you like to come to the show with us?

4. We may/will test the new car next week. We haven't decided yet.

5. You would/might want to check the show timings next time. I don't like missing the first half hour of the movie!

6. Dad can/may write about fifty pages in one day.

7. Could/may you have a happy Diwali.

8. May/will I take this chair?

9. My mother will/would do nothing but worry about my grandfather's health.

10. Arun will/would have called if his phone was working.

11. Even at that time Karan could/shall tell that Nisha was not well.

12. You can/should never interrupt elders when they are talking.

13. Shall/could I consider these final?

14. The workmen will/can install the system tomorrow morning for sure.

15. Would/can you like to think about it tonight?

16. Amit would/can have cooked dinner if the electricity would not have gone off.

17. Let me know if you can/should come in the evening. I will make the arrangements accordingly.

18. You could/shall not use mobile phones in the classroom.

19. I can/might have finished the assignment last night if I hadn't fall asleep.

20. Can/would you like to wait here till the doctor is free?

II. Complete the following sentences using the appropriate modal.

1. I _____ be in time for the wedding. (possibility)

2. Rita _____ have been on time if the traffic was not so much. (possibility)

3. My grandmother _____ be here next month. (certain future)

4. Vivek _____ play the piano very well. (ability)

5. _____ we take a break for a tea session now or later? (polite advice)

6. _____ this be a great start for you. (wishes)

7. You _____ want to see the traffic limit before speeding again. (disapproval)

8. You _____ see the principal tomorrow morning. (possibility)

9. Srishti _____ turn 21 next Sunday. (certain future)

10. _____ you like some more sugar? (question)

Choose the correct option to fill in the blanks with present, past or past participle forms of the verbs.

1. The dancer _____ well at the function.
   (a) Dances   (b) danced
   (c) dance   (d) dancing

2. A light rain _____ yesterday.
   (a) Fall   (b) fallen
   (c) falls   (d) fell

3. They _____ behind the bus.
   (a) ran   (b) Run
   (c) runs   (d) none

4. Terrorist's _____ WTC by hijacking aero planes.
   (a) Attack
   (b) Has been attacking
   (c) Attacked
   (d) All of these

5. I have been reading the book you lent me but I _____ (not/finish) it yet.
   (a) haven't finished
   (b) haven't finished
   (c) am not finishing
   (d) have not been finishing

🕐🕐🕐

Adverbs

Learning Objectives : In this chapter, students will learn about:
- ✓ Different types of adverbs

CHAPTER SUMMARY

An adverb is that word which tells you more about another word like a verb, an adjective, a clause or even another adverb.

Simple Adverb

Indefinite adverbs are the words that tell us more about verbs, adjectives or any other words. There are eight kinds of indefinite adverbs. The examples of these adverbs are given in the table below.

I. Adverb of Time: When you want to give more information about the time when something has happened.

II. Adverb of Place: These are words which give us more information about where something has taken place.

III. Adverb of Manner: The way that something has happened.

IV. Adverb of Degree or Adverb of Quantity: The extent to which something happens or takes place.

V. Adverb of Order or Condition: The way something is felt.

VI. Adverb of Number or, Adverb of Frequency: These are words which tell us how many times some event takes place.

VII. Adverb of Cause (Reason) and Effect: These are words which give us the connection between the reason why something happens and the result of that occurrence.

VIII. Adverb of Assertion (Affirmation) or Negation: These are words which help us understand whether something will take place or not.

TRIVIA

The symbol "&" is called an "ampersand", and is a version of the Latin word "et", which means "and".

Interrogative Adverb

The interrogative adverb is used to ask questions of different kinds in a sentence. Whenever you ask a question, you are using an interrogative adverb.

Let us try to understand the difference between the simple/indefinite adverbs and interrogative verbs.

S.No.	Adverb	Simple/Indefinite Adverb	Interrogative Adverb
1	Adverb of Time	I will watch the game today.	When will you go to the market?
2	Adverb of Place	My sister lives in Saket.	Where will she meet us?
3	Adverb of Manner	She was dancing beautifully.	How was the performance?
4	Adverb of Number	She always runs in the morning.	How often does she calls?
5	Adverb of Quantity/ Degree	I partially understand.	How much time do you need?
6	Adverb of Cause and Effect	It was raining, therefore he was late.	Why didn't you finish your work on time?
7	Adverb of Affirmation or Negation	He is definitely coming today.	When will he come today?
8	Adverb of Condition	He is feeling happy today.	How are you feeling today?

Relative Adverb

The third major classification of adverbs is the Relative Adverb. It is the Adverb that joins two clauses of a sentence together.

Examples:

We know the movies which she likes.

Here, the two classes are: 'We know the movies' and 'She likes'; 'which' is the word (adverb) which tells us the relation between the two clauses and hence is called the relative clause.

MUST REMEMBER

➡ An adverb is that word which tells you more about another word like a verb, an adjective, a clause or even another adverb.

➡ Indefinite adverbs are the words that tell us more about verbs, adjectives or any other words.

➡ The interrogative adverb is used to ask questions of different kinds in a sentence.

➡ Relative Adverb is the Adverb that joins two clauses of a sentence together.

PRACTICE EXERCISE

I. Read the following passage and identify the correct adverb.

It was already 9 o'clock (Adverb of time) and we were a little (Adverb of manner) late for the wedding reception that we were going to. There was a lot of traffic, therefore (1. _____) we were late by an hour. It was the wedding of the daughter of a friend of my father. The wedding was at a (2. _____) banquet hall in South Delhi. The bride and groom live in London (3. _____) and they had flown down to Delhi (4. _____) to get married. There was a lot of tasty (5. _____) food and great music. There was a live (6. _____) band and rides for kids. There were four (7. _____) kinds of cake but I had about five (8. _____) pieces of chocolate cake which (9. _____) I like better (10. _____) than any other. I always (11. _____) have chocolate cake. Dad asked me, "Are (12. _____) you having fun?" and I said, 'absolutely (13. _____)!' I wish I could go to weddings everyday (14. _____) Mummy lets me eat a lot (15. _____) of sweets and dad only says good (16. _____) things about me to everyone he meets. I get to wear good (17. _____) clothes and get to stay up late (18. _____ _____)! The only thing I don't like very much (19. _____) is when my mother's friends pull my cheeks. Thankfully that did not happen today (20. _____)

II. Read the following sentences and fill in the blanks with one of the options given below.

1. _____ does the team meet for cricket practice? We meet every Sunday at *7 am*
   (a) Where (place)
   (b) When (time)
   (c) How (manner)
   (d) How often (time)

2. _____do I open this box? There is a latch on the other side.
   (a) When (time)
   (b) How often (time)
   (c) Where (place)
   (d) How (manner)

3. _____ does this dress cost? It costs rupess 3000.
   (a) How much (quantity)
   (b) Where (place)
   (c) How long (time)
   (d) When (time)

4. _____ do you want to have dinner? Let's go to McDonald's?
   (a) How much (quantity)
   (b) Where (place)
   (c) How long (time)
   (d) How (manner)

5. _____ will you get the result? Tomorrow, I think.
   (a) How often (number)
   (b) Why (cause and effect)
   (c) Where (place)
   (d) When (time)

6. _____is your mother doing now? She is much better after taking the medicines.
   (a) How (manner)
   (b) How (condition)
   (c) How many (number)
   (d) How much (degree)

7. _____ is she staying this time? She is staying in Jaisalmer.
   (a) How many (number)
   (b) Where (place)
   (c) Are (condition)
   (d) When (time)

8. _____ is her wedding? It is day after tomorrow.
   (a) How often (number)
   (b) Where (place)
   (c) How much (degree)
   (d) When (time)

9. _____ gifts did she get on her birthday? She got almost 30 gifts!
   (a) Where (place)
   (b) How often (number)
   (c) How many (number)
   (d) How much (degree)

10. I understand that you like the movie but _____ times can you watch it!
    (a) How many (number)
    (b) Where (place)
    (c) How (manner)
    (d) How often (number)

HOTS

Form the correct sentences based on the hints given in brackets with each sentence.

1. The class begins at 11/on the high-way. (adverb of time)

2. The Rhino lives in strong/Assam. (adverb of place)

3. I partially agree/stupidly that we should call him right away! (adverb of affirmation and negation)

4. The French fries were still crunchy/on time (adverb of manner)

5. He is tall when/therefore he does not need a ladder. (adverb of cause and effect)

🕐🕐🕐

Adjectives

Learning Objectives : In this chapter, students will learn about:
- ✓ Different types of adjectives

CHAPTER SUMMARY

Adjectives are the words that are used to describe the kind of nouns and pronouns and to quantify and identify them.

Examples:

Rajan was wearing a red shirt.

Here 'red' is an adjective as it is describing the noun 'shirt'.

There are five rooms in the house.

Here 'five' is also an adjective because it is conveying the quantity/the number of noun 'rooms', answering the question 'how many rooms?'.

Kinds of Adjectives

Adjectives can be divided into five categories:

Adjectives of Quality

These adjectives are used to describe the nature of a noun. They show the characteristics of the noun by answering the question 'what kind'.

Examples:

Mr Mukherjee is an <u>honest</u> man.

Adjectives of Quantity

These adjectives show the amount or the approximate amount of the noun or pronoun. They do not provide exact numbers; rather they tell us the amount of the noun in relative or whole terms.

Examples:

<u>Many</u> people came to visit the fair.

> **TRIVIA**
>
> A word, phrase or sentence that is the same both backwards and forwards is called a Palindrome. Common examples are civic, radar, level, rotor, and madam.

Adjectives of Number

These adjectives are used to show the number of nouns and their place in an order. There are three different sections within adjectives of number; they are:

(i) **Definite Numeral Adjective:** The adjectives which clearly denote an exact number of nouns or the order of the noun.

One, Two, Twenty, Thirty-Three etc. are known as Cardinals.

First, Second, Third, Seventh etc. also known as Ordinals.

Example:

<u>Two</u> men were talking about the incident.

(ii) **Indefinite Numeral Adjective:** The adjectives which do not give an exact numerical amount but just give a general idea of the amount.

Some, Many, Few, Any, Several, All etc.

Example:

There were many people present at the gathering.

(iii) Distributive Numeral Adjective: The adjectives that are used to refer to individual nouns within the whole amount.

Either, Neither, Each, Another, Other etc.

Example:

<u>Every</u> student was given a pen, a pencil and a packet of biscuit.

Demonstrative Adjectives

These adjectives are used to point out or indicate a particular noun or pronoun. This, That, These and Those are demonstrative nouns.

Examples:

<u>That</u> bag belongs to Shyam.

I really like <u>those</u> shoes.

Interrogative Adjectives

These adjectives are used to ask questions about nouns or in relation to nouns. They are - Where, What, Which and Whose.

Examples:

<u>Whose</u> pen is this?

<u>Which</u> assignment did you submit?

MUST REMEMBER

➡ Adjectives are the words that are used to describe the kind of nouns and pronouns and to quantify and identify them.

➡ Adjectives of Quality are used to describe the nature of a noun.

➡ Adjectives of Quantity show the amount or the approximate amount of the noun or pronoun.

➡ Adjectives of Number are used to show the number of nouns and their place in an order.

➡ Demonstrative Adjectives are used to point out or indicate a particular noun or pronoun.

➡ Interrogative Adjectives are used to ask questions about nouns or in relation to nouns.

Choose the correct option and fill in the blanks.

1. We saw _____ animals at the zoo.
   (a) much
   (b) many
   (c) Both (a) and (b)
   (d) none of these

2. How _____ oranges did you put in the box?
   (a) much
   (b) many
   (c) Both (a) and (b)
   (d) none of these

3. There isn't _____ sugar in my coffee.
   (a) much
   (b) many
   (c) Both a and b
   (d) none of these

4. I don't have _____ friends.
   (a) much
   (b) many
   (c) Both (a) and (b)
   (d) none of these

5. The old man hasn't got _____ hair on his head.
   (a) much
   (b) many
   (c) Both (a) and (b)
   (d) none of these

6. I've packed _____ bottles of water.
   (a) much
   (b) many
   (c) Both (a) and (b)
   (d) none of these

7. I didn't get _____ sleep last night.
   (a) much
   (b) many
   (c) Both (a) and (b)
   (d) none of these

8. How _____ fruit do you eat everyday?
   (a) much
   (b) many
   (c) Both (a) and (b)
   (d) none of these

9. Can you please buy _____ apples?
   (a) a few
   (b) a little
   (c) Both (a) and (b)
   (d) none of these

10. We need _____ water.
    (a) a few
    (b) a little
    (c) Both (a) and (b)
    (d) none of these

11. I have _____ money left.
    (a) a few
    (b) a little
    (c) Both (a) and (b)
    (d) none of these

12. I take _____ sugar with my coffee.
    (a) a few
    (b) a little
    (c) Both (a) and (b)
    (d) none of these

13. We had _____ pints of beer there.
    (a) a few
    (b) a little
    (c) Both (a) and (b)
    (d) none of these

14. You have _____ time left.
    (a) a few
    (b) a little
    (c) Both (a) and (b)
    (d) none of these

15. There are _____ chairs in the room.
    (a) a few
    (b) a little
    (c) Both (a) and (b)
    (d) none of these

16. He only spent _____ dollars there.
    (a) a few
    (b) a little
    (c) Both (a) and (b)
    (d) none of these

17. I have _____ interest in classical music.
    (a) Little
    (b) Less
    (c) Both (a) and (b)
    (d) None of these

18. I have _____ faith in him.
    (a) little
    (b) less
    (c) Both (a) and (b)
    (d) none of these

19. We need _____ furniture in this dance hall than in the big one.
    (a) little
    (b) less
    (c) Both (a) and (b)
    (d) None of these

20. You have to drink _____ coffee.
    (a) little
    (b) less
    (c) Both (a) and (b)
    (d) none of these

1. An adjective of quality describes the _____ of a noun.
   (a) characteristics   (b) quantity
   (c) output   (d) none of these

2. We use an interrogative adjective to
   (a) ask question   (b) point
   (c) characteristics   (d) none of these

3. A possessive adjective shows
   (a) belonging   (b) characteristics
   (c) point   (d) none of these

4. Jupiter is the largest planet in the solar system. What is the adjective in it?
   (a) Jupiter   (b) the
   (c) largest   (d) planet

5. I used to drive _____ car.
   (a) a blue old German
   (b) an old German blue
   (c) an old blue German
   (d) old blue a German

Contractions

Learning Objectives : In this chapter, students will learn about:
- ✓ Concept of Contraction

CHAPTER SUMMARY

A shortened form of a word or group of words, with the missing letters usually marked by an apostrophe is called contraction.

Contractions are commonly used in speech and in colloquial forms of writing.

TRIVIA

"Underground" is the only word in the English language that begins and ends with the letters "und."

Standard Contractions in English

Contraction	Original
are not	aren't
cannot	can't
could not	couldn't
did not	didn't
does not	doesn't
do not	don't
had not	hadn't
has not	hasn't
have not	haven't
he had, he would	he'd
he will, he shall	he'll

he is, he has	he's
I had, I would	I'd
I will, I shall	I'll
I am	I'm
I have	I've
is not	isn't
it is, it has	it's
let us	let's
must not	mustn't
shall not	shan't
she had, she would	she'd
she will, she shall	she'll
she is, she has	she's
should not	shouldn't
that is, that has	that's
there is, there has	there's
they had, they would	they'd
they will, they shall	they'll
they are	they're

they have	they've	who will, who shall	who'll
we had, we would	we'd	who are	who're
we are	we're	who is, who has	who's
we have	we've	who have	who've
were not	weren't	will not	won't
what will, what shall	what'll	would not	wouldn't
what are	what're	you had, you would	you'd
what is, what has	what's	you will, you shall	you'll
what have	what've	you are	you're
where is, where has	where's	you have	you've
who had, who would	who'd		

MUST REMEMBER

➡ A shortened form of a word or group of words, with the missing letters usually marked by an apostrophe is called contraction.

Choose the correct contraction for the underlined words in each sentence.

1. <u>I am</u> going to the school.
   (a) I'am   (b) I'm
   (c) I'would   (d) None of these

2. <u>He is</u> driving his car.
   (a) He's   (b) He'is
   (c) He'll   (d) None of these

3. <u>She is</u> singing her favourite song.
   (a) She'is   (b) She'll
   (c) She's   (d) None of these

4. <u>It is</u> a huge cave.
   (a) It's   (b) Its
   (c) It'll   (d) 'It

5 <u>You are</u> very smart.
   (a) You's   (b) You'are
   (c) You're   (d) None of these

6. <u>We are</u> friends.
   (a) We're
   (b) We'are
   (c) We'll
   (d) None of these

7. <u>They are</u> going to climb that mountain.
   (a) They'are   (b) They're
   (c) They'r   (d) None of these

8) <u>I am</u> a student.
   (a) I'll
   (b) I'm
   (c) I' am
   (d) None of these

9. <u>That is</u> my house.
   (a) That'll   (b) That's
   (c) That'hv   (d) None of these

10. <u>Those are</u> rose bushes.
   (a) Those're   (b) Those'are
   (c) Those'hv   (d) None of these

11. <u>Who is</u> this?
   (a) Who'is   (b) Whois'
   (c) Who's   (d) None of these

12. <u>Where is</u> the book?
   (a) Where's   (b) Where'is
   (c) Where'll   (d) None of these

13. <u>Where are</u> we going tomorrow?
   (a) Where'is
   (b) Where're
   (c) Where'are
   (d) None of these

14. <u>I had</u> been to Chicago.
   (a) I'll   (b) I'had
   (c) I'd   (d) None of these

15. <u>You would</u> get that bed for the same price.
   (a) You'll   (b) You'd
   (c) You'could   (d) None of these

16. <u>You had</u> gone to the store.
   (a) You'd   (b) You'ad
   (c) You'il   (d) None of these

17. <u>I would</u> be there on time.
   (a) I'll   (b) I'would
   (c) I'd   (d) None of these

18. I <u>cannot</u> go there.
   (a) Can't
   (b) Cann't
   (c) Can'ot
   (d) None of these

19. They <u>are not</u> coming today.
   (a) Aren't   (b) are'not
   (c) areno't   (d) None of these

20. <u>I will</u> be there on time.
   (a) I'will
   (b) I'd
   (c) I'll
   (d) None of these

Fill in the blanks with the appropriate contractions:

1. _____ have to finish your work today. It has to be submitted tomorrow.
   (a) You'd   (b) You'll
   (c) You've   (d) You're

2. If it hurts you so much I promise, I _____ do it again.
   (a) isn't   (b) won't
   (c) can't   (d) don't

3. We _____ neglect our duties towards our elders.
   (a) mustn't   (b) must'nt
   (c) needn't   (d) shan't

4. Sarita _____ think of ignoring the duties that were assigned to her by her boss.
   (a) weren't   (b) don't
   (c) couldn't   (d) aren't

5. _____ reading Taslima Nasreen's book.
   (a) She'll   (b) She'd
   (c) She've   (d) She's

Articles

Learning Objectives : In this chapter, students will learn about:
✓ Different Articles and their usage

CHAPTER SUMMARY

An article is a word that modifies or describes a noun. It is used before the noun to show whether it refers to something specific or not. So, articles can also be described as a type of adjectives as they also tell us something about the nouns.

Types of Articles

There are two types of articles in the English language. They are as follows:

Definite Article

Definite means to be clear, exact or obvious about something. It is called definite because it is used in relation to a particular thing or person. 'The' is the definite article in the English, which is used to refer to particular nouns, the identities of which are known. The definite article indicates that the noun is specific. The speaker talks about a particular thing.

Examples:

The watch is lost. (watch is certain entity)

The dog barked at me and ran away. (dog is already known)

Indefinite Article

Indefinite means something which is not clear, obvious or exact. 'A' and 'An' are called indefinite articles because the identity of the thing or person being spoken about is left unclear or indefinite. The indefinite article indicates that the noun is not someone or something in particular. The speaker talks about any one of that type of things.

Examples:

Do you have a pencil? (that means any ordinary pencil)

I want to have an apple. (that means an ordinary apple)

TRIVIA

The only word in English dictionary that sums up exactly 100 is "attitude".

Usage of Indefinite Articles

Indefinite articles 'a/an' are used as follows:

1. 'A' is used before a word beginning with a consonant sound.

   Example:

   A boy, a gym, a horse, a joke, a kite, a lion, a mirror, a noise, etc.

2. 'An' is used before a word beginning with a vowel sound. Vowel letters in the English alphabet are A, E, I, O, U.

   Example:

   An apple, an elephant, an idiot, an orange, an umbrella, etc.

   Note: The usage of articles is on the basis of sound and not only the letter the word starts with.

Examples:

An honest man.

A one-eyed dog.

3. We use 'a' and 'an' only before a singular noun. We can't use 'a' and 'an' before a plural noun.

Examples:

A book - correct

A books - incorrect

4. If the noun is modified by an adjective, the choice between a and an depends on the initial sound of the adjective that immediately follows the article.

Examples:

A beautiful umbrella

A European country

5. A/An is used to indicate membership in a group.

Examples:

I am a journalist.

She is an Indian.

Usage of Definite Article 'The'

1. Before the names of rivers, oceans and seas: the Ganga, the Indian Ocean

2. Before the major latitudes and longitudes globe: the Equator, the Tropic of Cancer

3. Before the geographical areas: the South East, the Asia Pacific

4. Before the deserts, forests, gulfs, and peninsulas: the Kalahari, the Sunderbans

Do not use 'the' before:

1. The names of most countries/territories: India, Brazil, Canada; however, the Netherlands, the Dominican Republic, the Philippines, the United States

2. The names of cities, towns, or states: Delhi, Sao Paolo

3. The names of streets: Callowhill Drive, Park Avenue

4. The names of lakes and bays: Lake Michigan, Lake Ontario; except while referring to a group of lakes - the Great Lakes

5. The names of mountains: Mount Everest, Mount Fuji except with ranges of mountains like the Andes or the Rockies or unusual names like the Matterhorn

6. The names of continents: Asia, Europe

7. The names of islands (Easter Island, Maui, Key West) except with island chains like the Andaman Islands, the Canary Islands

Omission of Articles

1. When you talk about things in general

Example:

I like birds.

Here, the speaker wants to imply that he/she likes any bird in general, and not a specific bird.

2. When talking about plural count nouns

Example:

Dogs are faithful animals.

3. When talking about non-count nouns

Example:

I love music.

4. When talking about specific days or holidays, geography, companies, languages.

Example:

I have bought candles for Diwali.

Here, the speaker is talking about the candles he has bought to use on the day of Diwali.

5. Articles are not used before countries, states, cities, towns, continents, single lakes, single mountains, etc.

Example:

I live in Canada.

6. When you talk about companies

Example:

Steve Jobs founded Apple.

7. When you talk about languages

Example:

I speak Hindi.

8. When you talk about places, locations, streets

    Example:

    I left my pen at home.

    However, there are specific places that do need the use an article.

    Example:

    The bank, the hospital, the post office, the airport, the train station, the bus stop, etc.

9. When you talk about sports and physical activities

    Example:

    I love to play cricket.

    She enjoys dancing.

10. When there is a noun + number

    Example:

    The train to Delhi leaves from platform 9.

11. When talking about academic subjects

    Example:

    I hate attending Mathematics classes.

MUST REMEMBER

➡ The definite article indicates that the noun is specific.

➡ The indefinite article indicates that the noun is not someone or something in particular.

PRACTICE EXERCISE

Choose the correct option and fill in the blanks.

1. Who is _____ girl with Rajkumar.
   (a) the   (b) a
   (c) a / the   (d) none

2. We need a secretary with _____ good knowledge of English.
   (a) a   (b) the
   (c) a / the   (d) none

3. We're having _____ terrible weather.
   (a) a   (b) the
   (c) a / the   (d) none

4. What did you do with _____ stereo I lent you?
   (a) a   (b) the
   (c) a / the   (d) none

5. Could you close _____ window?
   (a) a   (b) the
   (c) a / the   (d) none

6. My sister lives in _____ London.
   (a) a   (b) the
   (c) a / the   (d) none

7. Emily is excited about being _____ grandmother
   (a) a   (b) the
   (c) a / the   (d) none

8. Life would be much less stressful without _____ telephone.
   (a) a   (b) the
   (c) a / the   (d) none

9. _____ Giant Panda is in danger of becoming extinct.
   (a) a   (b) the
   (c) a / the   (d) none

10. Mother is in _____ hospital. She has got kidney trouble.
    (a) a   (b) the
    (c) a / the   (d) none

11. I am studying _____ life of Socrates.
    (a) a   (b) the
    (c) a / the   (d) none

12. He said that he wanted to become _____ engineer.
    (a) a   (b) an
    (c) the   (d) none

13. He remained _____ spinster all his life.
    (a) a   (b) the
    (c) a / the   (d) none

14. We have planted some roses in _____ garden.
    (a) a   (b) the
    (c) a / the   (d) none

15. 'What is that noise?' 'I think it is _____ airplane.'
    (a) a   (b) an
    (c) the   (d) none

16. Is there _____ water in the pot?
    (a) some   (b) any
    (c) the   (d) a

17. 'Lend me your pen, please.' 'I haven't got _____ pen.'
    (a) a   (b) the
    (c) a / the   (d) none

18. _____ whisky is made from barley.
    (a) A   (b) The
    (c) A / The   (d) none

19. I think there is _____ butter in the fridge.
    (a) some   (b) any
    (c) some/any   (d) the

20. The headmaster was talking to _____ parents.
    (a) a   (b) an
    (c) the   (d) none

Fill in the blanks by putting a/an/the and complete the story:

The Ant and The Grasshopper

Once upon ___ time, there lived ___ ant and ___ grasshopper in ___ grassy meadow. It was during ___ hot summer season when ___ ant was toiling hard by collecting wheat grains from ___ farmer's field. On ___ other hand, ___ grasshopper spent all his time in singing and dancing. He would frequently call ___ ant to join him in singing and dancing. However, ___ ant would ignore him and continue with her work. ___ ant said that she was saving some food for ___ cold season and recommended ___ grasshopper to follow ___ same. ___ grasshopper didn't pay heed to her words and continued singing and dancing merrily. Soon summer faded to autumn and autumn to winter. Out of cold, ___ grasshopper lost his interest in singing and making merry. He was cold and hungry and had no place to take shelter from ___ snow outside. Suddenly he remembered about ___ ant and visited her for some food and shelter. ___ grasshopper made ___ approach to her for some food and shelter. She gently asked him to sing somewhere else and earn his food and shelter. It is then, ___ grasshopper realized that he should have saved up enough for ___ winter instead of wasting his time being lazy during summer in singing and dancing around.

Prepositions

Learning Objectives : In this chapter, students will learn about:
✓ Different types of prepositions

CHAPTER SUMMARY

A preposition is word, which helps you understand the relationship between different words in a sentence to tell you more about the direction, location or the time.

Prepositions of time

The most common prepositions of time are: At, on and in

Examples:

She reached home at 9 pm

She reached home on Monday

She came home in the second week of July

Based on the examples above, we can understand that when 'at', 'on' and 'in' are used as prepositions of time, they are used to indicate the following things:

1. **At:** for the specific time of the day.

   Therefore, you can also say, 'at night', 'at the weekend', 'at present', 'at Diwali', 'at breakfast' etc.

2. **On:** to tell you the day or the date on which something happens

   More examples of the same are: 'on the '27th', 'on Friday morning' etc.

3. **In:** to indicate the longer/broader period in which an event takes place.

Other examples include: 'in the winters', 'in the 20th century', 'in the future', 'in 1971' etc.

'On' and 'In' are also prepositions which are used along with 'time' to indicate punctuality.

When you are 'on time' it means that you are punctual.

Example:

The football match began on time and finished on time.

When you are 'in time' it means that you have some time enough to complete an action.

Example:

I hope I am in time to see the beginning of the parade. (it means that you want to be there 'before' the parade begins so that you can see it. This means that to be 'in time' for something, you have to be there before the assigned time.'

Prepositions of place

The most common prepositions which indicate the place are 'in', 'on' and 'at'. These are the words which tell you where an object is placed or where an event takes place. Let's look at these examples to understand the preposition of place better.

In: You should always throw the trash in the waste basket.

On: You should never throw the trash on the ground.

At: The waste basket is kept at the back.

From the examples above we come to know that the preposition 'in' tell you when one object is in another object.

Examples:

Trash is 'in' the waste basket or 'window in the room,' 'parade in Delhi' or 'pencil in hand', 'in a queue', 'in the water', 'in the car', 'in the backseat of a car', 'in the sun' etc.

The preposition 'on' tells you when an object is placed on top of another object. 'hat on the head', 'clock on the wall', 'on a bus/train/plane', 'on the third floor',

 There are some other expressions like 'on the phone' - though you are not actually on top of the phone, this is just a way of saying it. Similar are the expressions, 'on a holiday', 'on the television', 'on the radio', 'on fire', 'on a diet', 'on contract' etc.

The preposition 'at' tells you the position of an object with respect to another object. 'waiting at the bus stop', 'at the top of the page', 'at the back of a building' etc. This is the preposition used for occasions and events. Like 'at the party', 'at the anniversary dinner' etc.

Examples:

There is soda 'in' the glass.

There is soda written 'on' the can.

I got this glass of soda 'at' the shop by the temple.

Look at the different ways that these prepositions are used:

'In' and 'At' – He is still 'in' bed 'at' his home. He was playing 'in' his room.

"I studied 'at' the university for three years" but "I am 'in' the university right now."

"I live 'in' Delhi" but "the train stops 'at' Delhi before reaching Agra".

(You use 'in' when you want to talk about places, cities but 'at' when they are a point in a journey.)

'I eat at the restaurant'. or 'I eat in the restaurant'.

(You can use both 'in' and 'at' for buildings)

Prepositions of direction

When to travel or move in direction, you use prepositions to denote and indicate which direction you are moving in.

You always go to and come to/from a place. You can also go into a room/building etc.

Go to/come from Chennai/bank/school/airport etc.

Move into the house. 'get into the car'

Directions

Click Here

You can also use the preposition 'in' with 'arrive' to indicate where one has come.

Example:

They 'arrive in' Russia by the morning flight.

The Preposition By

The last preposition we are going to discuss is 'By.' This is a preposition which is used in many different ways.

It is used to denote the 'manner' – would you like to pay by cash or by card?

Example:

I like travelling by train.

By can be used to denote location as well.

Example:

I live in the house by the lake.

By can be used to denote the time also.

Example:

I will meet you there by 7 pm.

By can also be used to denote the increase or decrease in something.

Example:

In the marathon, she won by 20 seconds.

MUST REMEMBER

➡ A preposition is word, which helps you understand the relationship between different words in a sentence to tell you more about the direction, location or the time.

➡ The most common prepositions which indicate the place are 'in', 'on' and 'at'.

I. **Choose the correct answer from the options given. These are all prepositions of time.**

1. I was on/in/at time for the inter-view.

2. She has just changed her job. She is now working at/on/in a bank.

3. The buses here are never in/on time. I always have to wait at least an hour.

4. The students had a party on/ in/ at Monday.

5. There is so much fog nowadays. If you take the train, you will not be able to reach in/at/time for the wedding.

6. You can get these fruits only at/on/in the summer.

7. She will call at/in/on time 6 am when she reaches London.

8. The Prime Minister is visiting Japan at/in/on March next year.

9. It is the premiere of the movie. Please be in/on/at time.

10. The shop opens at/on/in 10 am. We can get the things at that time.

II. **Complete the following sentences using 'in', 'at' or 'on' which are the prepositions for place.**

1. Did you draw that picture hanging _____the wall?

2. I will put the gift_____ a box before I wrap it.

3. We will meet them _____the cinema hall.

4. Eiffel tower is _____Paris.

5. There were no clouds _____the sky. We thought it was a good day for a picnic.

6. Write your name _____the top of the page.

7. She lives_____ the ground floor. You don't have to climb any stairs.

8. Put the letter _____ an envelope. I will post it tomorrow.

9. I like a lot of cheese _____ my pizza.

10. The door bell rang. Will you see who is _____ the door?

III. **Read the following sentences and see if the preposition used in the sentence is correct. If not, fill in the correct preposition.**

1. If you are looking for the magazine, it is by the backseat. Correct/incorrect.

2. I have never travelled by ship. Correct/incorrect.

3. If you are coming for Anjana's wedding, I will see you at the reception hall. Correct/incorrect.

4. I was looking for my mother and as always, she was at the kitchen. Correct/incorrect.

5. We could not get plane tickets so she had to travel on train. Correct/incorrect.

6. I love eating in the little restaurant by the museum. Correct/incorrect.

7. Should we stop at Alwar for a meal or should we drive straight to Shimla? Correct/incorrect.

8. I searched for my phone for ten minutes and ultimately found it on my pocket. Correct/incorrect.

9. I studied on the University of Delhi. Correct/incorrect.

10. This winter, the temperature has dropped by at least 5 degrees. Correct/incorrect.

(I) Underline the prepositions in this paragraph:

Gautam Buddha was born in 563 BC at Lumbini in Sakya Kshatriya clan of Kapilvastu on Vaiskha Purnima Day. His father Suddhodhana was the Saka ruler, his mother Mahamaya died after 7 days of his birth, so he was brought up by stepmother Gautami. He left home at the age of 29 years. He attained enlightenment at 35 years of age at Bodh Gaya under a pipal tree on the banks of Phalgu river on the 49th day of meditation.

(II) Fill in the blanks with suitable prepositions:

(1) The government of India has decided ___ celebrate the birthday ___ Netaji Subhash Chandra Bose, ___ 23rd January, as 'Parakram Diwas' every year. This day will be dedicated ___ honour and remember Netaji's selfless service ___ the nation.

(2) I love ___ keep my room neat and clean. My books and other study materials are ___ my table. My t-shirts are ___ the cupboard. The shoes ___ mine are ___ the shoe rack. There is a ceiling fan ___ my bed. I have a TV ___ the wall ___ the room. There is a big photograph ___ my parents ___ the TV.

(3) A greedy dog wandered ___ search for food. He stood ___ a meat shop. He stole a large piece ___ meat and ran away ___ it. He found a river ___ his way. There was a bridge ___ it. When he was crossing the bridge, he saw his own reflection ___ the water. As he thought that it was another dog. He wanted that piece ___ meat also. So he barked ___ his own reflection. He opened his mouth and the piece ___ meat fell ___ the water. Then he repented for his action.

(III) Which of the following are correct options?

A. The cat sprang upon the table.

B. I have been unwell by Monday.

C. He has been sleeping for the last three hours.

D. We sat over the ground.

(a) A and B are correct

(b) A and C are correct

(c) B and C are correct

(d) C and D are correct

Conjunctions

Learning Objectives : In this chapter, students will learn about:
- ✓ Usage of Conjunctions

CHAPTER SUMMARY

Conjunctions are the parts of speech and are used to connect words, phrases, clauses, or sentences.

Types of Conjunctions

Different types of conjunctions do various jobs within sentence structures. These include:

Subordinating Conjunctions

Also known as subordinators, these conjunctions join two parts of a sentence wusing the conjunctions:

After, Although, As, As soon as, Because, Before, By the time, Even if, Even though,

Every time, If, In case, Now that, Once, Since, So that, Than, The first time, Unless,

Until, When, Whenever, Whether or not, While, Why etc.

TRIVIA

The word "queue" is the only word in the English language that is still pronounced the same way when the last four letters are removed.

Coordinating Conjunctions

Also known as coordinators, these conjunctions coordinate or join two or more sentences, words, or other parts of speech which are of the same importance.

Some coordinating conjunctions are:

For, And, Nor, But, Or, Yet, So

Correlative Conjunctions

These conjunctions correlate, working in pairs to join phrases or words that carry equal importance within a sentence.

Some pairs of correlative conjunctions are:

As/as, Both/and

Either/or

Hardly/when

If/then

Just as/so

Neither/nor

Not only/but also

No sooner/than

Not/but

Rather/than

Scarcely/when

What with/and

Whether/or

In the following sentences, the conjunctions are italicized for easy learning.

- I tried to hit the nail *but* hit my thumb instead.

- I have two goldfishes <u>and</u> a cat.
- I'd like a bike <u>for</u> commuting to work.
- You can have either the peach ice-cream <u>or</u> the brownie sundae.
- <u>Neither</u> the black dress <u>nor</u> the gray one looks good on me.

- My dad always worked hard *so* we could afford the things we wanted.
- I try very hard to study <u>yet</u> I am not receiving good grades.

MUST REMEMBER

➡ A conjunction is a part of speech that is used to connect words, phrases, clauses, or sentences.

➡ Correlative Conjunctions correlate, working in pairs to join phrases or words that carry equal importance within a sentence.

Choose the correct option to fill in the blanks in each sentence.

1. My sister loves animals. She just brought a puppy _____ a kitten home with her.
   a But
   (b) Or
   (c) Yet
   (d) And

2. I'd like to thank you _____ the lovely gift that you gave me.
   (a) Or
   (b) For
   (c) And
   (d) Yet

3. I want to go for a hike _____ I have to go to work today.
   (a) But
   (b) Yet
   (c) Or
   (d) For

4. They do not smoke, _____ do they play cards.
   (a) And
   (b) Or
   (c) Nor
   (d) Yet

5. I'm getting good grades _____ I study every day.
   (a) Or
   (b) Yet
   (c) But
   (d) Because

6. _____ the basement flooded, we spent all day cleaning up.
   a After
   (b) Although
   (c) Before
   (d) Even If

7. I don't want to go to the movies _____ I hate the smell of popcorn.
   (a) Although
   (b) Because
   (c) Whenever
   (d) So that

8. I paid Larry, _____ garden design work is top-notch.
   (a) Whenever
   (b) Whose
   (c) After
   (d) If

9. _____ spring arrives, we have to be prepared for more snow.
   a. Because
   b. Until
   c. Although
   d. Now that

10. _____ the alarm goes off, I hit the snooze button.
    (a) As soon as
    (b) Because
    (c) Before
    (d) Now that

11. She is neither polite _____ funny.
    (a) Or
    (b) Nor
    (c) Not
    (d) Yet

12. _____ that is the case, _____ I'm not surprised about what's happening.
    (a) If/then
    (b) No sooner/than
    (c) Scarcely/when
    (d) Whether/or

13. Have you made a decision about _____ to go to the movies _____ not?
    (a) If/then
    (b) Either/or
    (c) Whether/or
    (d) What with/and

14. _____ had I put my umbrella away, _____ it started raining.
    (a) No sooner/than
    (b) If/then
    (c) What with/and
    (d) Neither/nor

15. This salad is _____ delicious _____ healthy.
    (a) Whether/or
    (b) Both/and
    (c) Scarcely/when
    (d) Rather/than

16. You need to put more effort into your work; _____, you won't get a passing grade.
    (a) Moreover
    (b) Otherwise
    (c) Unless
    (d) Instead

17. We wanted to spend the day at the beach; _____, it rained so we stayed home.
    (a) Moreover
    (b) Unless
    (c) However
    (d) Additionally

18. She is a very smart girl; _____, it's not at all surprising that she gets such good grades.
    (a) Again
    (b) Besides
    (c) Contrarily
    (d) Therefore

19. Javed is a millionaire; _____, his brother Jeremy is always flat broke.
    (a) In contrast
    (b) Accordingly
    (c) Again
    (d) Likewise

20. He felt he couldn't tell the truth about what happened; _____, he lied.
    (a) In contrast
    (b) Likewise
    (c) Undoubtedly
    (d) Instead

In each question, select the correct option that combine the two sentences withoutchanging their meaning.

1. Do you want coffee now? Do you want it later?
   (a) Do you want coffee now and later?
   (b) Do you want coffee now but not later?
   (c) Do you want coffee now or later?
   (d) Do you want now but also coffee later?

2. Roja did not meet Shalini. She did not meet Malini.
   (a) Roja either did not meet Shalini or Malini.
   (b) Roja neither met Shalini or Malini.
   (c) Roja neither met Shalini and Malini.
   (d) Roja met neither Shalini nor Malini.

3. Sneha wants money. Sneha wants fame.
   (a) Sneha wants money or fame.
   (b) Sneha wants both money as well as fame.
   (c) Sneha wants money nor fame.
   (d) Sneha wants both money and fame.

4. I bought a neck-tie. I bought a pair of glasses.
   (a) I bought a pair of glasses as well as a neck-tie.
   (b) I bought both a pair of glasses but also a neck-tie.
   (c) I bought a pair of glasses and too, a neck-tie.
   (d) I bought a pair of glasses or a neck-tie.

5. This is not the time for playing. This is the time for studying.
   (a) This is neither the time for playing nor the time for studying.
   (b) This is the time for studying not for playing.
   (c) This is neither the time for playing but for studying.
   (d) This is either the time for playing or for studying.

Learning Objectives : In this chapter, students will learn about:
✓ Usage of tenses in English

CHAPTER SUMMARY

Tenses are the forms of verb (action words) which tell us the time at which the action takes place. There are three ways in which you can talk about time:

1. When you talk about things which have already happened. This is called the **past tense.**
2. When you talk about things which are taking place right now at the time when you are talking about them. This is called the **present tense**.
3. When you talk about the things which are going to take place after sometime, in the future. This is called the future form.

Examples:

I went to the theatre yesterday. (past tense)

I go to school every day (present tense)

I will go to the market tomorrow (future form)

These three tenses have four further types each. See the following examples of the four types of present tense:

- **I walk:** Simple present (simply mentioned, we do not know whether the action, here walking, is complete or not and when.

- **I am walking:** Present continuous (hints that the action, walking, is still going on and has not been completed at the time at which you are talking about it)

- **I have walked:** Present perfect (The action, walking, has completed at the present moment when you are talking about it)

- **I have been walking:** Present perfect continuous (this shows that the action, walking, has been going on for some time and at the present moment it has not completed)

Let's discuss the simple tenses in more detail.

TRIVIA

The word "triskaidekaphobia" means "fear of Friday the 13th". It also means "superstition about the number thirteen" in general.

Simple Present Tense

Tense is the form of the verb in its core form changed only according to whether it is used in the first person or second. It is used in the following scenarios:

1. To make statements about the things which are happening at the present moment.

Example:

Here is the lotion.

It is also used in commentaries instead of the present continuous.

Example:

Dhoni hits the ball and it goes for a six!

2. To state universal and general truths.

Example:

The sun rises from the east. Even though the sun might not be rising at the exact moment when you are talking about it, but it is a universal truth which never changes.

It is also used for quotations, as they never change.

Example:

Premchand talks about the division among the citizens.

3. To talk about habits.

Example:

I go to school every day.

4. It can replace the simple future tense under two conditions:

(a) It can also be used to talk about time tables and schedules in the future.

Example:

The train arrives at 4 pm.

(b) When there is clause of time in the future.

Example:

If it stops, just call the plumber.

5. Sometimes the simple present replaces the simple past in stories for dramatic effect.

Example:

Meena rises slowly from the chair and looks out the window, only to be astonished.

Simple Past Tense

This tense is used to indicate an action which has been completed in the past. It is usually accompanied by an indication of the time when it was completed. The simple past tense is created by adding '-ed' to the base form of the regular verbs.

Verb (Basic Form)	Verb (Simple Past Tense)
Watch	Watched
Walk	Walked
Play	Played
Talk	Talked

There are some irregular verbs as well for which the past tense forms do not follow the 'ed' rule. You just have to learn the past tense of these verbs. Some examples of irregular verbs forming past tense are:

Verb Form (Irregular)	Verb (Past Tense)
Read	Read
See	Saw
Teach	Taught
Give	Gave

The simple past tense is also used to indicate habits in the past.

Examples:

She always read in the library. (here read is the simple past tense of the irregular verb read)

He watched TV every night from 6-8 pm.

Simple Future tense

The simple future has many uses like the simple present. We can create the simple future tense in two ways:

1. By using the auxiliary verb 'will.'

Examples:

I will eat my dinner in another half hour.

2. By using the auxiliary verb 'going to'.

Example:

She is going to open the box now.

Some of the places where simple future tense is used are:

1. When we talk about things which we think will happen in the future.

   Example:

   She will probably come tomorrow.

2. When we declare what we are going to do in the future.

   Example:

   It' getting late. I will call my mother and tell her that I won't be in time for dinner.

3. When we state facts about the future, especially when we cannot control them.

   Example:

   The train hopefully will arrive in time tomorrow.

4. We use the 'going to' form of the future tense when we make a guess about the future based on some things which happen in the present or the past.

Example:

She is going to call. She called at the same time yesterday.

5. We also use the 'going to' form of the verb when we talk about something that is going to take place in the immediate future.

Example:

Be careful, the cracker is going to burst!

MUST REMEMBER

➡ Tenses are the forms of verb (action words) which tell us the time at which the action takes place.

➡ Tense is the form of the verb in its core form changed only according to whether it is used in the first person or second.

➡ The simple past tense is also used to indicate habits in the past.

PRACTICE EXERCISE

I. Choose the correct option to com-plete the following sentences.

1. The university opens/opened on the 17th July every year.

2. Kusum called/will call me as soon as he comes.

3. The water is already boiled it will spill over/spills over if you don't turn off the heat.

4. I talks/talked to him yesterday.

5. Fish swim/will swim in water.

6. The next train is/was at 6:15 am tomorrow morning.

7. Shakespeare said/says, what's in a name?

8. It will take us/takes us twenty more minutes to reach there, have patience.

9. Please be quiet, the chief guest is going to speak/speak in a moment.

10. I heated/will heat the food for her yesterday.

11. I will see if the letter comes/came today.

12. The sails/ship sailed out of the harbour in time last week.

13. Sania will get/gets the medal for us in the coming Olympics.

14. I have decided that I went/am going to go to Ladakh this summer.

15. My alarm ring/rings at 5:30 every morning.

II. Complete the following sentences with the correct form of the verb.

1. I _____ milk every night. (present continuous – habit)
   (a) Drink   (b) Drank
   (c) Will drink   (d) Drinks

2. The Bhagavat Gita says, your duty is to _____ your work as best as you can. (Present – quote)
   (a) Will finish   (b) Finished
   (c) Finish   (d) Finishes

3. It is _____ cats and dogs, the clouds are all black. (future – prediction)
   (a) Rains   (b) Rained
   (c) Going to rain (d) Rain

4. The parade _____ at 6 am every year on 26th January. I watch it. (present – habit)
   (a) Will begin   (b) Began
   (c) Begin   (d) Begins

5. I just spoke to her. She _____ upset. (past)
   (a) Seem
   (b) Seemed
   (c) Will seem
   (d) Is going to seem

6. Every mother _____ her child. (present – statement)
   (a) Loves   (b) Loved
   (c) Love   (d) Will love

7. We have just started from Shimla. We _____ Delhi after ten hours. (future)
   (a) Reached   (b) Will reach
   (c) Reach   (d) Reaches

8. I always _____ an umbrella here. (present – habit)
   (a) Will carry   (b) Carried
   (c) Carry   (d) Carrying

9. Let's quickly go inside. It's _____ any minute now.
   (a) Going to rain (b) Rained
   (c) Rain   (d) Rains

10. I think she _____ a song, she is a good singer. (future – prediction)
    (a) Sings   (b) Will sing
    (c) Sang   (d) Sing

11. Here _____ the cake! (present – statement)
    (a) Was   (b) Will be
    (c) Is going to be (d) Is

12. If she _____, we will go to the museum. (present – clause of time and condition)
    (a) Came
    (b) Will come
    (c) Come
    (d) Comes
13. Renu _____ maths. (present – habit)
    (a) Like
    (b) Liked
    (c) Likes
    (d) Will like
14. We _____ the new car last month. (simple past)
    (a) Booked
    (b) Will book
    (c) Books
    (d) Book
15. Sita _____ at ram and falls in love with him. (present – dramatic)
    (a) Looked
    (b) Looks
    (c) Will look
    (d) Look

HOTS

Read the passage given below and complete the sentences using the verb given in the brackets:

Water in the sea and on the ground constantly __ (1) __ (evaporate) due to heat of the sun. Water __ (2) __ (get) converted into vapour which __ (3) __ (go) upwards in the atmosphere. Water vapours then __ (4) __ (condense) on the dust particles to form clouds. When clouds __ (5) __ (go) up, they condense into water which __ (6) __ (come) down again as rains. __ (7) __ (you know) what __ (8) __ (happen) to this water? All of it __ (9) __ (not seep) into earth. Most of it __ (10) __ (collect) in the sea and other reservoirs of water on land. It evaporates again, __ (11) __ (rise) in the sky and __ (12) __ (convert) into rainwater.

⏰⏰⏰

Jumbled Words and Punctuations

16

CHAPTER SUMMARY

In the questions based on jumbled words, the students are required to understand the jumbled phrases, comprehend the meaning implied, and put the sentence in order.

Examples:

The first doctor a diagnosis makes an illness of (Jumbled words)

The doctor first makes a diagnosis of the illness. (Ordered words)

He or she what then kind decides of treatment needed is (Jumbled words)

Then he or she decides what kind of treatment is needed. (Ordered words)

Proper sentences are made up of words. In jumbled sentences words are not arranged in a proper order. These words are jumbled. The student is expected to look at the jumbled words, comprehend the meaning implied, and arrange the words in proper order to make a meaningful sentence.

- That / lived in / halls / l dreamt / I / marble

Answer: I dreamt that I lived in marble halls.

Rearrange the words and make a meaningful sentence.

1. Said / the child/ that / leave /the mother/ alone / could not / she.

   The mother said that she could not leave the child alone.

2. After / they / had / the theatre / begun/ reached / show / the.

   They reached the theatre after the show had begun.

3. Pond/jumped/the dog/into the

   The dog jumped into the pond.

4. The bag/against/threw/the wall/He.

   He threw the bag against the wall.

5. Shakespeare / greater/ all / poets / than / is / other/the.

   Shakespeare is greater than all the other poets.

6. Bridge / over / is a / there / the stream.

   There is a bridge over the stream.

7. Pay/you/on time /dues/must/the.

   You must pay the dues on time.

8. Hockey / evening / we/ a / match / last / play.

   We played a hockey match last evening.

9. Last/met/Sunday/her/you.

   You met her last Sunday.

10. Metal / useful / is a / steel / very.

    Steel is a very useful metal.

Jumbled Words

If you were given the letters 'T L I N L E G N I T E' to unscramble, or un-jumble, if you will, those letters to reveal the word 'INTELLIGENT'

Below given is a list of jumbled words and their meaningful words

1. I O L N	=	LION
2. A R O P R T	=	PARROT
3. O R S H E	=	HORSE
4. V A Y E H	=	HEAVY
5. H I L G T	=	LIGHT
6. E N E I C S C	=	SCIENCE
7. E P A R P	=	PAPER
8. R S T A	=	STAR
9. A F N	=	FAN
10. I N G E S H L	=	ENGLISH
11. E RU PS E	=	RUPEES
12. C A E R	=	RACE
13. T H K C N E I	=	KITCHEN
14. S M T S Y E	=	SYSTEM
15. A B S A S D R O M A	=	AMBASSADOR
16. K O C R F	=	FROCK
17. TO U R C	=	COURT
18. C R E O F	=	FORCE
19. W A D F R	=	DWARF
20. L O E O W N	=	WOOLEN
21. GTN H I	=	NIGHT
22. A H W O D S	=	SHADOW
23. O S D R L E I	=	SOLDIER
24. Y E M N E	=	ENEMY
25. N M I R G O N	=	MORNING
26. R O B E R H T	=	BROTHER
27. T O C P E K	=	POCKET
28. V S E R E L A	=	SEVERAL
29. N O S I O P	=	POISON
30. I T H A F F L U	=	FAITHFUL

Punctuation

Learning English punctuation is an important skill of acquiring a complete grammatical knowledge. Punctuation is used to create sense, clarity and stress in sentences. It means the right use of putting in points or stops in writing. The following are the principal stops:

(1) Full Stop or Period (.)

(2) Comma (,)

(3) Semicolon (;)

(4) Colon (:)

(5) Note of Interrogation or Question Marks (?)

(6) Note of Exclamation or Exclamation Marks (!)

(7) Dash (_)

(8) Parenthesis ( )

(9) Inverted Commas or Quotation Marks (" ")

TRIVIA

"Rhythms" is the longest English word without the normal vowels, a, e, i, o, or u.

Full Stops and Commas

Full stops are used at the end of a sentence to inform the reader that the sentence is finished and that he should take a moment before reading the next one.

Examples:

1. Honesty is the best policy.
2. Please shut the door.
3. The teacher is teaching the pupils.

A comma informs the reader to pause before continuing the sentence. Unlike a period, the sentence is not over but simply being paused for a moment.

Example: Health, wealth and peace go together.

Question and Exclamation marks

Like a full stop, a question mark finishes a sentence. Unlike a full stop, a question mark turns the sentence into a question rather than a statement.

Example: What are you writing in your copy? He said, "Who is there?"

An exclamation point also ends a sentence like a full stop, but the sentence is turned into an exclamation rather than a simple statement. Readers should read a sentence with an exclamation mark with excitement.

Example: Bravo! We have won the match. Alas! His dog is dead.

Colons and Semicolons

A semicolon connects two free-standing but related sentences where the conjunction has been left out. Semicolons are typically used before introduction words such as namely, however, therefore, that is, for example or for instance.

Example: God gave her peace; her land reposed.

A colon is used before a sentence that expands on the previous one. Colons are often used before listing items.

Example: Shakespeare says: "Sweet are the uses of adversity."

Apostrophes and Parentheses

An apostrophe is used in a contraction in place of the letter that has been removed. "It's" uses an apostrophe to replace the "i" in "is." "It's" is a contraction of "it is." Parentheses are used to enclosed clarifying statements. Someone might use parentheses (if they thought it was necessary) to help clarify or expand on a sentence. If parentheses are used in a narrative, the sentence must also make sense if the words in the parentheses were not included.

Dash

It is used to indicate an abrupt stop or change of thought or to resume a scattered subject.
Example: Friends, companions, relatives---all deserted him.

MUST REMEMBER

➡ Punctuation is used to create sense, clarity and stress in sentences. It means the right use of putting in points or stops in writing.

➡ Full stops are used at the end of a sentence to inform the reader that the sentence is finished and that he should take a moment before reading the next one.

➡ Unlike a full stop, a question mark turns the sentence into a question rather than a statement.

➡ A semicolon connects two free-standing but related sentences where the conjunction has been left out.

PRACTICE EXERCISE

Arrange the words given in each sentence to form a meaningful sentence and choose the correct option from the alternatives.

1. ship violently the storm rocked the
   - (a) The ship rocked the storm violently.
   - (b) The storm rocked the ship violently.
   - (c) Violently the storm rocked the ship
   - (d) None of these

2. masterpiece artist painstakingly the his worked at
   - (a) The artist painstakingly worked at his masterpiece.
   - (b) The masterpiece painstakingly worked at the artist.
   - (c) Painstakingly the masterpiece worked at the artist.
   - (d) None of these

3. Gift free a Dad offered firm by the was.
   - (a) Firm was offered a free gift by the dad.
   - (b) Dad was offered a gift free by the firm.
   - (c) Dad was offered a free gift by the firm.
   - (d) None of these

4. I read paper in the burglar been caught had the that.
   - (a) The burglar had been caught I read in the paper.
   - (b) I read in the paper that the burglar had been caught.
   - (c) In the paper I read that the burglar had been caught.
   - (d) None of these

5. nightfall began crickets the at their piercing calls.
   - (a) At nightfall the crickets began their piercing calls.
   - (b) The crickets began piercing calls at their nightfall.
   - (c) The crickets began their piercing calls at nightfall.
   - (d) None of these

6. Wore a hat he of coconut made fiber his on head.
   - (a) He wore a hat made of coconut fiber on his head.
   - (b) He wore a hat on his head made of coconut fiber.
   - (c) A hat made of coconut fiber he wore on his head.
   - (d) None of these

7. parts many coffee popular in world the is very of.
   - (a) In many parts of the world coffee is very popular.
   - (b) Coffee is very popular in many parts of the world.
   - (c) In many parts coffee is very popular of the world.
   - (d) None of these

8. Cave could explore not they torch the without a
   - (a) They could not explore the cave without a torch.
   - (b) Without a torch they could not explore the cave.
   - (c) The cave they could not explore without a torch.
   - (d) None of these

9. The storm shed damaged the was during.
   - (a) The shed was damaged during the storm.
   - (b) During the storm the shed was damaged.
   - (c) The shed damaged was during the storm.
   - (d) None of these

10. The dog James talking sat next to himself to
    - (a) James sat talking to himself next to the dog.
    - (b) The dog sat next to James talking to himself.
    - (c) James sat next to the dog talking to himself.
    - (d) None of these

11. That lived in halls I dreamt I marble
    (a) In marble halls I dreamt that I lived.
    (b) I dreamt I lived that in marble halls.
    (c) I dreamt that I lived in marble halls.
    (d) None of these

12. are given to cannot be people who quarrelling happy
    (a) People who are given to quarrelling cannot be happy.
    (b) People cannot be happy who are given to quarrelling.
    (c) who are given to quarrelling people cannot be happy.
    (d) None of these

13. as if was in a hurry he worked he
    (a) As if he was in a hurry he worked.
    (b) As if he worked he was in a hurry.
    (c) He worked as if he was in a hurry.
    (d) None of these

14. What you if you I you will get want do as say
    (a) What you want you will get if you do as I say
    (b) You will get what you want if you do as I say.
    (c) If you do as I say you will get what you want
    (d) None of these

15. She was of her youth at that time, in the prime
    (a) At that time, she was in the prime of her youth.
    (b) At that time, prime of her youth she was in.
    (c) Both (a) and (c)
    (d) None of these

HOTS

Form a meaningful sentence.

1. Twice/day/brush/teeth/a/your
   (a) Brush your teeth twice a day.
   (b) Twice a day your teeth brush.
   (c) A day twice brush teeth your.
   (d) Your teeth twice a day brush.

2. Sky/in/are/blue/birds/flying
   (a) Sky blue in birds are flying.
   (b) flying sky in blue are birds.
   (c) Birds are flying in blue sky.
   (d) None of these

3. A/story/I/be/narrating/will/tomorrow
   (a) I story will be a narrating tomorrow.
   (b) I will be narrating a story tomorrow.
   (c) A story will be narrating I tomorrow.
   (d) Will tomorrow be a story I narrating.

4. God / pray/to/daily/we/should
   (a) To daily we should pray God.
   (b) Pray we & God should to daily.
   (c) We daily to should pray God.
   (d) None of These

5. Doctor/apple/an/keeps/a/the/away/day
   (a) A doctor an day keeps the apple away.
   (b) An apple a day keeps the doctor away.
   (c) A doctor an apple keeps the day away.
   (d) away an apple keeps the doctor a day.

🕐🕐🕐

SECTION 2
READING
COMPREHENSION

Tips on Reading Comprehension

When you read a text, you get to know a lot of things that you did not know earlier. If you follow the below given steps to answer the reading comprehension passages then you will be able to do them very well.

1. Always keep an open mind when you read. You will learn new things.

2. Read the questions before you read the passage. This way, you will already know which questions you need to answer.

3. Make a note of all the important points in the passage.

4. It is always a good idea to write down any word or information that you don't know. Ask someone about this later.

5. Once you have answered questions about a passage, you will most likely remember it for a long time. Make sure that you understand everything. Use a dictionary if needed.

6. If you do not have a dictionary and need to understand a word, see how it is used and guess the meaning. You can always tell if it is a noun or a verb; if it is positive or negative etc.

Read the following poem by Ogden Nash and answer the questions which follow:

This is Going to Hurt Just a Little Bit

One thing I like less than most things is sitting in a dentist chair with my mouth wide open.

And that I will never have to do it again is a hope that I am against hope hopen. Because some tortures are physical and some are mental,

But the one that is both is dental.

It is hard to be self-possessed

With your jaw digging into your chest.

So hard to retain your calm

When your fingernails are making serious alterations in your life line or love line or some other important line in your palm;

So hard to give your usual effect of cheery benignity

When you know your position is one of the two or three in life most lacking in dignity.

And your mouth is like a section of road that is being worked on.

And it is all cluttered up with stone crushers and concrete mixers and drills and steam rollers and there isn't a nerve in your head that you aren't being irked on.

Oh, some people are unfortunate enough to be strung up by thumbs.

And others have things done to their gums,

And your teeth are supposed to be being polished,

But you have reason to believe they are being demolished.

And the circumstance that adds most to your terror

Is that it's all done with a mirror,

Because the dentist may be a bear, or as the Romans used to say, only they were referring to a feminine bear when they said it, an ursa,

But all the same how can you be sure when he takes his crowbar in one hand and mirror in the other he won't get mixed up, the way you do when you try to tie a bow tie with the aid of a mirror, and forget that left is right and vice versa?

And then at last he says That will be all; but it isn't because he then coats your mouth from cellar to roof

With something that I suspect is generally used to put a shine on a horse's hoof.

And you totter to your feet and think. Well it's all over now and afterall it was only this once.

And he says come back in three months.

And this, O Fate, is I think the most vicious circle that thou ever sentest,

That Man has to go continually to the dentist to keep his teeth in good condition when the chief reason he wants his teeth in good condition is so that he won't have to go to the dentist.

1. What is the one thing that the poet likes less than any other thing in the world?

    Answer: The poet likes sitting in a dentist's chair less than anything else in the world.

2. Which is the torture which is both physical and mental?

    Answer: The one torture which is both physical and mental is dental.

3. When is it hard to be self-possessed according to Nash?

    Answer: According to Nash, it is hard to be self-possessed when your jaw is digging into your chest.

4. What are the fingernails making a serious alterations in?

    Answer: The fingernails are making serious alterations in lifeline, or loveline or any other line in the poet's palm.

5. What does the mouth look like when you are sitting in a dentist's chair?

    Answer: The mouth looks like a road that is being worked in a dentist's chair.

6. What are the construction machines that Nash lists in the poem?

    Answer: Nash lists stone crushers, concrete mixers, steam rollers and drills.

7. When does the poet feel that his teeth are being demolished?

    Answer: The poet feels that his teeth are being demolished when they are being polished.

8. What is the circumstance that adds most to your terror?

    Answer: The circumstance that adds most to your terror is that it is all done in a mirror.

9. Why is the poet scared that the dentist is working with the mirror?

    Answer: The poet is scared that the dentist is working with a mirror because the dentist might forget that left is right and vice versa.

10. What is the most vicious circle according to Ogden Nash?

    Answer: The most vicious circle according to Ogden Nash is that we go to the dentist to keep our teeth in good condition and the reason why we want our teeth to be good condition is so that we don't have to go to the dentist.

Comprehension 1

Read the following story and answer the questions which follow.

There was once an ant. His name was Anand. He was always joyful, energetic and hardworking. As a result, he was fit as a fiddle. Anand used to work at the sugar factory because he liked eating sweets a lot. He always wanted to be near sweets. He used to reach office on time, finish his work on time and happily come back home in time to see his favourite TV shows. He was happy as a clam in mud at high tide.

Anand had a friend, Gautam. Gautam was a grasshopper and even though they were friends, they were both as different as chalk and cheese. He hardly ever worked and spent most of his evenings at Anand's place for dinner. He was also very jealous of Anand as he thought that Anand had an easy job. He always said that if he had such an easy job, he would have made a lot of money too. That is the reason why the grasshopper kept on becoming green with envy.

Summers were alright but winters were very tough on the Gautam. Even Anand could only save so much grain for the winter months. If he would have shared all his grains with Gautam then both of them would have died of hunger.

Once when Anand had refused to give Gautam any food, Gautam decided to go to the king of the jungle, the lion. Gautam said to the lion, "Is this not unfair? I am starving here and Anand is sitting comfortably at home with a hot supper? There should be a law which ensure that every body gets food when hungry."

The lion smiled and said, "You reap what you sow, since you didn't work all year, you are hungry. Since Anand has worked so hard,

he has all the comforts! This is justice! I can't take the fruits of his labour away from him. He has earned his reward." Gautam had to go home without any free food but with an important lesson.

1. You have read the following idioms in the passage, based on your understanding, write down their meanings:

   (a) Happy as a clam in the mud in high tide.

   _____
   _____
   _____

   (b) As different as chalk and cheese.

   _____
   _____
   _____
   _____

   (c) Become green with envy.

   _____
   _____
   _____

   (d) Reap what you sow.

   _____
   _____
   _____

   (e) Fit as a fiddle.

   _____
   _____
   _____

2. Answer the following questions on the basis of the story you have read above.
   (a) Where did Anand work?

   _____
   _____
   _____

   (b) Did he like working there?

_____

_____

_____

(c) Was the Gautam like Ananda?

_____

_____

_____

(d) Where did Gautam take most of his dinners?

_____

_____

_____

(e) How did Anand prepare for the winters?

_____

_____

_____

(f) Who did Gautam go to with his complaint?

_____

_____

_____

(g) What did Gautam tell the king?

_____

_____

_____

(h) Did the king agree with Gautam?

_____

_____

_____

(i) What did the king tell Gautam?

_____

_____

_____

(j) What did you learn from this story?

_____

_____

_____

Comprehension 2

Read the following dialogue and answer the questions which follow.

Gopal: Did you know that it was Revathy's birthday yesterday?

Anish: No, I was busy with my cricket practice all morning.

G: That's right, you guys are preparing for the zonal finals. How is the practice coming along?

A: We're doing well. I think we have a good chance.

G: Great! I hope you guys win the zonal match this year! We havn't won in the last three years.

A: We are working very hard. We should be able to get the cup this year. Did you go to Revathy's party?

G: Yes, I did. It was a great party. We all went paintball shooting in the afternoon and then for lunch at McDonald's.

A: That sounds great! I have never been paintball shooting. Did you guys go to the outlet near Sec-18?

G: Yes. Her parents had rented the whole place for two hours and we played in two teams. Revathy was the captain for one of the teams and Aisha was the captain for the other.

A: That sounds great. Who won?

G: Revathy won. We all were happy that she won during her birthday celebrations. After wards, we went to McDonald's and she cut a cake there. We were also gifted with little toys which come with happy meal.

A: It sounds like I missed out on a lot of things. Was Rohan there? He left the practice early saying that he had to go to a party. I think he must have met you guys.

G: Yes. He joined us only at McDonalds. He came with us to Revathy's house and he even won the first round of games that we played on her play station.

A: What else did you guys do?

G: There was a very nice clown as well. He played a lot of tricks and made us laugh a lot. There was a magician who showed us a lot of magic tricks. He made a rabbit disappear and showed us a handkerchief which was about a mile long!

A: I saw a trick like that once in a magic show I saw with my dad in Mumbai once. We also saw a lot of gymnasts who swayed so high on the trapeze that it looked like they were hanging from the sky.

G: I would love to see that! I will ask my dad to take me to Mumbai to see that show.

A: I think they have that show in Delhi as well. I saw a similar thing in youtube some days ago. My brother showed it to me.

G: Let's see it now? I also want to see the highlights of the football match from last night. Have you finished your homework?

A: I finished it two hours ago. I am completely free. Even my mother gave me permission to use the internet for an hour.

1. Whose birthday was it yesterday?

   _____
   _____
   _____

2. Why didn't Anish go to Revathy's birthday party?

   _____
   _____
   _____

3. Does the cricket team have a good chance in the Zonal finals?

   _____
   _____
   _____

4. How long has the cricket team not won?

_____
_____
_____

5. Did Gopal go to Revathy's party?

   _____
   _____
   _____

6. Where did the kids go in the afternoon?

   _____
   _____
   _____

7. Where did the kids go for lunch?

   _____
   _____
   _____

8. Has Anish ever been paintballing?

   _____
   _____
   _____

9. Which paintball outlet did the guys go to?

   _____
   _____
   _____

10. How long had Revathy's parents rented the paintball outlet?

    _____
    _____
    _____

11. Who were the captains for the two paintball teams?

    _____
    _____
    _____

12. Who won the paintball competition?

_____

_____

_____

13. What kind of toys did the kids get at McDonald's?

_____

_____

_____

14. Was Rohan at Revathy's birthday party?

_____

_____

_____

15. Where did he join the party?

_____

_____

_____

16. Who won the first round of games on the play station?

_____

_____

_____

17. Who made the kids laugh a lot at Revathy's birthday party?

_____

_____

_____

18. What tricks did the magicians show?

_____

_____

_____

19. Who looked like they were hanging from the sky?

_____

_____

_____

20. What do Anish and Gopal decide to do online?

_____

_____

_____

Comprehension 3

Read the following article and answer the questions which follow based on the passage:

World Cup 2015: Indian team defeat the Pakistan team.

Virat Kohli scored a great century to help defending champions, India, begin the World Cup with a 76-run victory over rivals Pakistan.

India's win earns national pride in what was thought to be the most watched cricket match of all time, with an estimated television audience of one billion, and extends their World Cup record against Pakistan to six wins from as many matches.

It was also a splendid way to begin the defence of a trophy India won in 2011 and represents their first competitive win since the tour of Australia in November. Pakistan, winners when the tournament was last held in Australia and New Zealand 23 years ago, can take heart from the way they tried, but their chase of the score was poor. After all the hype, the action was intriguing, rather than exciting.

Making first use of an excellent pitch on a very hot day, India's innings was made successful by Kohli's calm accumulation all around the wicket. He hit eight fours in his 126-ball stay.

The right-hander made Pakistan pay for dropping his catch twice, the first a tough chance in the deep to Yasir Shah when on only three, the second a more straightforward edge behind to Umar Akmal on 76.

When the 26-year-old attacked Shahid Afridi's bowling to long-on to score a 22nd ODI hundred he became the first man to score a century in his opening match of a World Cup tournament on two occasions. Only Sachin Tendulkar has more centuries than him now.

Dhawan, who controlled his attacking instincts supported Kohli a lot and Raina, who repeatedly heaved through the leg side in his 56-ball knock, was also a lot of help. However, after Kohli edged Sohail to Umar, Pakistan put up a good fight through fast bowler Sohail, who demonstrated consistency of length and intelligent changes of pace. India managed to score only 27 runs in their final five overs as five wickets fell. Sohail was responsible for taking four of these five wickets.

1. Which year's World Cup does the article talk about?

   _____
   _____
   _____

2. How much did Virat Kohli score?

   _____
   _____
   _____

3. What was the estimated television audience for this match?

   _____
   _____
   _____

4. When did India win this trophy?

   _____
   _____
   _____

5. How many fours did Kohli score?

   _____
   _____
   _____

6. Is Kohli a right-hander or a left-hander?

   _____
   _____
   _____

7. How many times did Pakistan drop Kohli's catch?

   _____
   _____
   _____

8. How many centuries does Kohli have in ODIs as per the passage?

   _____
   _____
   _____

9. How many times has he scored centuries in the opening match of World Cup?

   _____
   _____
   _____

10. Who is the only other cricketer who has more centuries than him as per the passage?

    _____
    _____

11. Who were the other two cricketers who supported Kohli?

    _____
    _____

12. How much did Raina score?

    _____
    _____
    _____

13. Which Pakistani bowler showed consistency in length and intelligence in changes of pace?

_____

_____

_____

14. How many runs did India score in the final five overs?

_____

_____

_____

15. How many out of the last five wickets did Sohail take?

_____

_____

_____

Comprehension 4

Read the following diary entry and answer the questions given at the end.

Dear diary,   15th May 2014

One of my cousins got married yesterday and we all went to a farmhouse for the wedding. The farmhouse was so grand that we were busy just exploring the place for about an hour!

Sonu kept on saying that if we looked closely enough, we might just find some hidden treasures like in the book the Treasure Island. Only we would find it in a farmhouse, not in an island. Diary, do you remember Sonu? She is the cousin of mine who lives in Kolkata and eats fish with everything. Even with biscuits! I always tell her that she should live in the water if she likes fish so much. She can catch all the fish she wants and eat as much as she wants. She reads a lot and always asks us to pretend like we are the famous five from a book she has read. I tell her that six kids can't be famous five and she just says that out of all six, Deepti will not be famous as she still gets her shoe laces tied by her mum. So the rest of the five will be the famous five.

The whole farmhouse was decorated with lights of all sorts. There were light which were hanging, there were lights which were floating and lights which were stuck on to things. From a distance it looked like the whole place was full of holes and there was a bright light inside which was filtering out of these small holes.

My cousin, Preeti didi, got married to a German man and lives in Germany now. She got a lot of chocolates for all of us. In fact she sent us chocolates with the wedding invitation. We told her that she should get married every year. Then we will have such chocolates every year. She also gave us posters of an old painter guy whose name my mother made me memorize. His name was Gogh. I know it sounds like Gogh but it is actually called Guff! I don't understand English sometimes.

There was also a lot of other good food in the wedding but I overate. I always overeat because I don't want to miss out on anything good but end up with a stomach ache the next day. I have a stomach ache even right now. I will go and take some medicine and give you the details of the wedding tomorrow. Bye!

1. What is the date on which the diary entry has been written?

_____
_____
_____

2. Where did the writer go for the wedding?
_____
_____

3. How long did it take to explore the farmhouse?
_____
_____

4. Which book did Sonu talk about which has hidden treasures?
_____
_____

5. Where does Sonu live?
_____
_____

6. What does Sonu eat with everything?
_____
_____

7. Why does the writer tell Sonu that she should live in the water?
_____
_____

8. What does Sonu ask everyone to pretend?
_____
_____

9. Why can't they be famous five?

10. Why does Sonu feel that Deepti cannot be famous?
_____
_____

11. What kinds of lights does the writer talk about?
_____
_____

12. What is the name of the writer's cousin?
_____
_____

13. Who did the writer's cousin marry?
_____
_____

14. What came along with the wedding invitation?
_____
_____

15. What did the writer ask Preeti didi to do every year?
_____
_____

16. What did she give along with the chocolates and the invitations?
_____
_____

17. What was the name of the old painter guy?

_____

_____

_____

18. What does the writer always do?

_____

_____

_____

19. What is the problem that the writer is facing at the time of writing the diary?

20. When will the writer tell the diary about the details of the wedding?

_____

_____

_____

SECTION 3
SPOKEN AND WRITTEN EXPRESSIONS

Tips for Good Conversation

Some of the usual phrases which we use in everyday conversation depend on who we are talking to. The way we say the same thing, changes with the person being addressed. Let's look at the way we would change the same thing according to the person being addressed.

1. Let us begin with introductions.
   (a) If you are addressing someone you don't know very well or since very long then you will address them in a formal manner. The introduction might resemble the following conversation:
   Paul: Hello. Let me introduce myself, my name is Paul.
   Sidharth: Hi Paul. I am Sidharth. How are you?
   Paul: I am good. Thanks for asking. How are you?
   Sidharth: I am good too. Thanks.
   (b) If however, Paul and Sidharth were friends and Paul was introducing someone new, the conversation might look something like:
   Paul: Hi Sidharth! How are you? This is Kavya.
   Sidharth: I am great! How are you? Hi Kavya!
   (c) If you are introducing someone to a group, then you will perhaps use one of the following sentences:
   Hello everyone, I would like to introduce Sheetal. She is the new accountant.
   Hi everyone, can I introduce Sheetal, our new accountant?
   Hey everyone, This is Sheetal, our new accountant.
   (d) When you have to greet someone, you use phrases like:
   Good Morning/Good afternoon/ Good evening
   Hi there.

Long time no see.
How are you? It's good to see you.

2. Now that we know how to introduce someone new, let us look at some ways of making requests. Even in this regard, the way you approach someone will depend on what your relationship with them is.

Let us look at the following examples.
- Can you help me with _____?
- Would it be possible for you to _____?
- Could you possibly _____
- Will you be able to _____?
- When you respond to a request you usually do it in the following ways:
- Okay
- Sure, no problem.
- I would love to.
- I can help you with
- Sorry, I would not be able to
- I can't help you with
- I will not be able to

When you do something wrong and have to apologise for it, you use the following phrases to do the same:
- I am sorry for
- I must apologise for
- I wish to apologise for
- I shouldn't have
- It is my fault that
- I am sorry for
- Please forgive me for
- Please accept my apology for

When you accept someone's apology, the phrases you generally use are:
- Don't mention it.
- It is quite alright.
- Forget about it.
- Don't fret about it.
- It doesn't matter.
- Its okay.
- I understand.
- No harm done.

PRACTICE EXERCISE

I. Which occasion do the following belong to?

1. Hi, this is Ranjan –
2. I would love to –
3. I am sorry for –
4. Good evening –
5. It's okay –
6. Can I introduce Ria –
7. Forget about it –
8. Sorry, I would not be able to –
9. No harm done –
10. It's good to see you –
11. Hi Parul, how are you? –
12. Sure, no problem –
13. Please forgive me for –
14. Good afternoon –
15. Don't mention it –

II. Choose the best response from the options given below:

1. Why did you run away?
   (a) I was frightened by the sound of thunder.
   (b) Were you tired?
   (c) Were you happy?
   (d) None of the above.

2. I would like to finish my assignment today.
   (a) Would you be able to?
   (b) Won't you be able?
   (c) Will you be able to?
   (d) None of the above.

3. Rakshak is so boring, I don't want to invite him.
   (a) I must invite him.
   (b) I understand your problem, but you will have to.
   (c) You will invite him.
   (d) Both (b) and (c)

4. Where is the boss going during vacation?
   (a) I don't have any idea.
   (b) I really wonder where he is going?
   (c) Don't you think where he is going!
   (d) All of the above.

5. Could I borrow some storage devices from you?
   (a) Why do you need them for?
   (b) What do you need them for?
   (c) What do you need them?
   (d) Both (b) and (c)

6. Haven't you put on weight recently?
   (a) No, there isn't.
   (b) Yes, I did
   (c) Yes, I have.
   (d) Both (a) and (b)

7. Ali: "My friend doesn't work very hard"
   Riya: "_____?"
   Ali: "Of course I do!"
   (a) Do you?
   (b) Don't you?
   (c) Have you?
   (d) All of these.

8. Ann: "Where's Rajghat?"
   Jim: "_____."
   Ann: "Can you tell me where Rajghat is?"
   (a) Repeat
   (b) I can't understand.
   (c) I beg your pardon.
   (d) I could not understand.

9. How much are these mangoes?
   (a) One kilo for twenty five rupees.
   (b) Twenty five rupees a kilo.
   (c) One kilo in twenty five rupees.
   (d) One kilo on twenty five rupees.

10. Are you sure you will win?
    (a) I am afraid I will.
    (b) I think I will
    (c) I'm sure I will.
    (d) All of these.

SECTION 4
ACHIEVERS' SECTION

Key Chart

Reflexive Pronouns Used with Personal Pronouns

Usually, reflexive pronouns are used with other pronouns. Reflexive pronouns are used when the subject is doing an action by itself. This is especially helpful when using third person plural.

Personal Pronouns	Reflexive Pronouns
I	Myself
You	Yourself
He	Himself
Her	Herself
It	Itself
We	Ourselves
They	Themselves

Common Errors with Reflexive Pronouns

1. There might be some situations where reflexive pronouns sound confusing if it is used at the beginning of the sentence.
    (a) Ourselves were introduced by us. ✗
    (b) We introduced ourselves. ✓
    (c) Myself was cheered up by me. ✗
    (d) I cheered myself up. ✓

2. The most common mistake is to use a reflexive pronoun instead of a personal pronoun (I, me, he, she).

Example:

(a) If you think you have any doubts, just ask myself. ✗

(b) If you think you have any doubts, just ask me. ✓
-   The first sentence is grammatically incorrect as the reflexive pronouns do not replace personal pronouns.

-   In sentence two, the sentence uses a personal pronoun.

Present Indefinite Tense

Affirmative Sentences: Subject + Verb I (s/es) + Object

Negative Sentences: Subject + do / does + not + Verb + Object

Interrogative Sentences: Do / Does + Subject + Verb I + Object

Affirmative	Negative	Interrogative
I eat.	I do not eat.	Do I eat?
He plays.	He does not play.	Does he play?
It rains.	It does not rain.	Does it rain?
He writes.	He does not write.	Does he write?

Past Indefinite Tense

Affirmative Sentences: Subject + Verb II + Object

Negative Sentences: Subject + did + not + Verb I + Object

Interrogative Sentences: Did + Subject + Verb I + Object

Affirmative	Negative	Interrogative
I ate.	I did not eat.	Did I eat?
He played.	He did not play.	Did he play?
It rained.	It did not rain.	Did it rain?
He writes.	He did not write.	Did he write?

Future Indefinite Tense

Affirmative Sentences: Subject + Will/Shall + Verb + Object

Negative Sentences: Subject + Will/Shall not + Verb I + Object

Interrogative Sentences: Will/Shall + Subject + Verb I + Object

Affirmative	Negative	Interrogative
I Shall eat.	I shall not eat.	Shall I eat?
He will play.	He will not play.	Will he play?
It will rain.	It will not rain.	Will it rain?
He will write.	He will not write.	Will he write?

Common Mistakes in Noun

1. Do not interchange collective nouns used for people with animals or with one type of animal and another.

Examples:

1. A swarm of bees attacked the man with the cane.
2. A herd of bees attacked the man with the cane. (herd- a group of cattle)

2. Collective nouns can be treated as singular or plural.

Examples:

1. The committee was formed in 1916.
2. The committee is having lunch.

Indefinite Pronoun

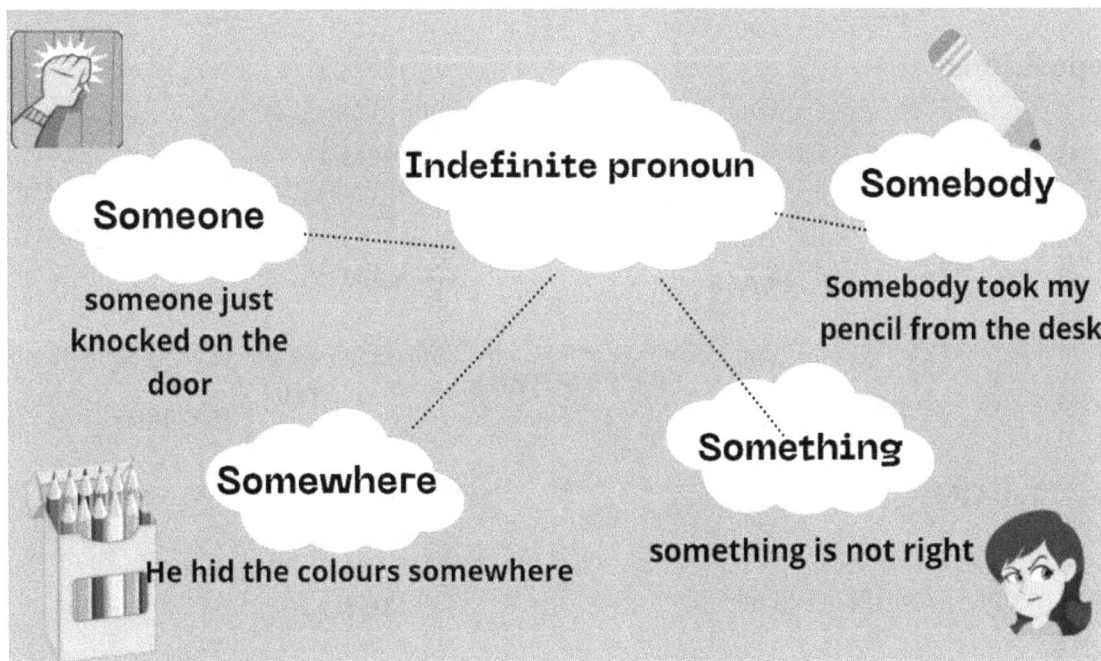

Indefinite pronoun

Someone
someone just knocked on the door

Somebody
Somebody took my pencil from the desk

Somewhere
He hid the colours somewhere

Something
something is not right

Personal Pronoun

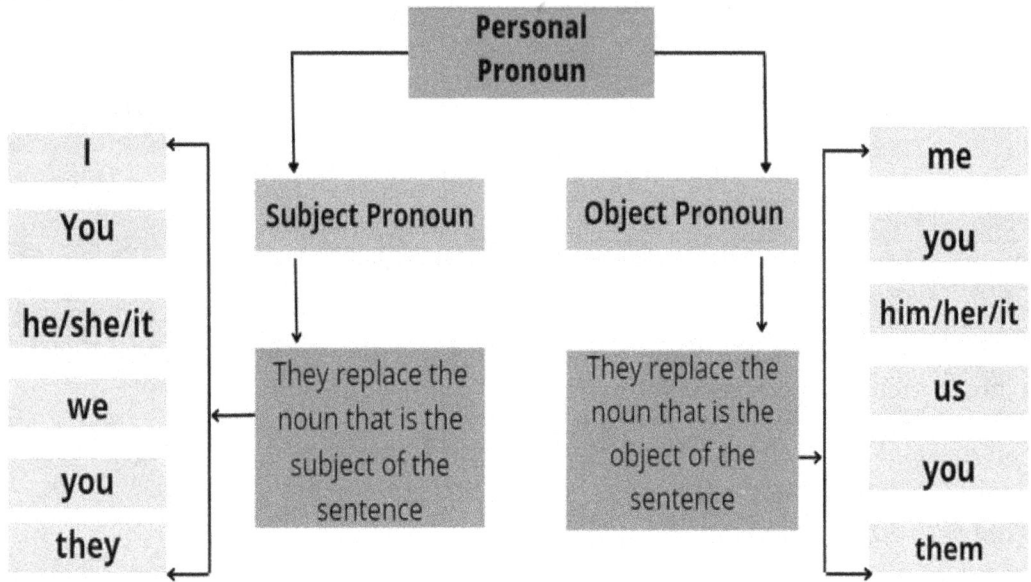

Prepositions

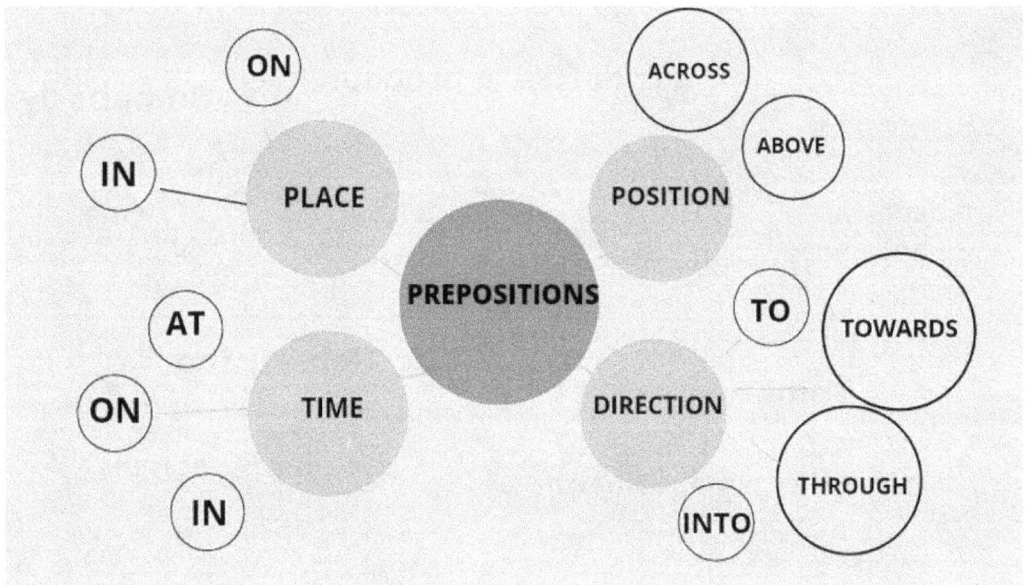

Common Mistakes in Preposition

1. A preposition is used to link a verb to the rest of the sentence. However, you have to choose the exact preposition based on the verb that comes before it.

Examples:

1. She should listen **to** our opinion.

2. Sanjay has been busy **with** work recently.

3. Employees are not allowed **to** smoke here.

Each of the prepositions in bold are the only suitable prepositions to follow the highlighted verbs that go before them. For example, it would be grammatically wrong to say "listen of" or "busy for."

2. A noun or pronoun (object of the preposition) must follow a preposition. A verb cannot be the object of a preposition.

Examples:

- The cake was for her. (The preposition for is followed by the pronoun her)
- The cake was for eat. (The preposition for is followed by the verb eat.)
- Place the plate by the bowl. (The preposition by is followed by the noun bowl.)

- Place the place by the washing. (The preposition by should not be followed by the verb washing.)

3. Do not use prepositions at the end of a sentence. Since prepositions are followed by a noun, they should not appear at the end of a sentence.

Examples:

- The table is where I put my alarm clock **on**.
- Where does he go **to**?

Conjunctions and its Meaning

Word	Meaning	Example
For	To give reasons	I purchased new books because I love reading.
And	In order to add information	She baked cake and cookies.
Nor	To add negative information	He didn't join us nor did he inform us.
But	To show contrast	The shop is open but there are no chocolates
Or	To give another choice	You can enjoy with us or stay home.
Yet	To show contrast	I was enjoying in party yet I wanted to go back.
So	To give result	He missed his bus so he was late today.

Comparative and Superlative Degrees

Following are the rules for Forming of Comparative and Superlative Degrees:

1. The adjective forms in the comparative have the ending–'er' to the word.

For a positive degree, the word is created by adding **'est'**.

Examples:

Positive	Comparative	Superlative
Tall	Taller	Tallest
Kind	Kinder	Kindest
Sweet	Taller	Tallest
Bold	Bolder	Boldest

Cold	Colder	Coldest
Fast	Faster	Fastest
Great	Greater	Greatest
Young	Younger	Youngest
Small	Smaller	Smallest
Strong	Stronger	Strongest

Some Common Descriptive Sounds relating Humans.

In a story, characters express their thought or emotions with words. Sometimes their action also is accompanied by sounds words that tell you more about the current situation of the character.

Examples

Sounds	Expression
argh	Expression of annoyance.
babble	To utter meaningless sounds.
brr	Sound of shivering.
burp	Expel gas from the stomach.
clap	Sound made with palms together.
Gulp	Sound of swallowing
haha	Sound of laughter
hehe	High pitched laughter
munch	Chew noisily
shh	Sound of silencing
zzz	sleeping

Sounds Made by Objects

Describing objects in the sounds of objects whether they break, collide, shatter, etc.

Examples:

Sounds	Expression
Bang	The sound of an explosion
Beep-beep	Car horn
Clink	Sound of glass
Ding-dong	doorbell
Flutter	Sound of motion
Ring-ring	Phone ringing
thud	A big object falling
vroom	Sound o

Common Error for Adjectives

While using cardinal and ordinal together, make sure the ordinal precedes the cardinal.

Examples:

(a) The five first women will be given the opportunity. ✗

(b) The first five women will be given the opportunity. ✓

Modal Auxiliary

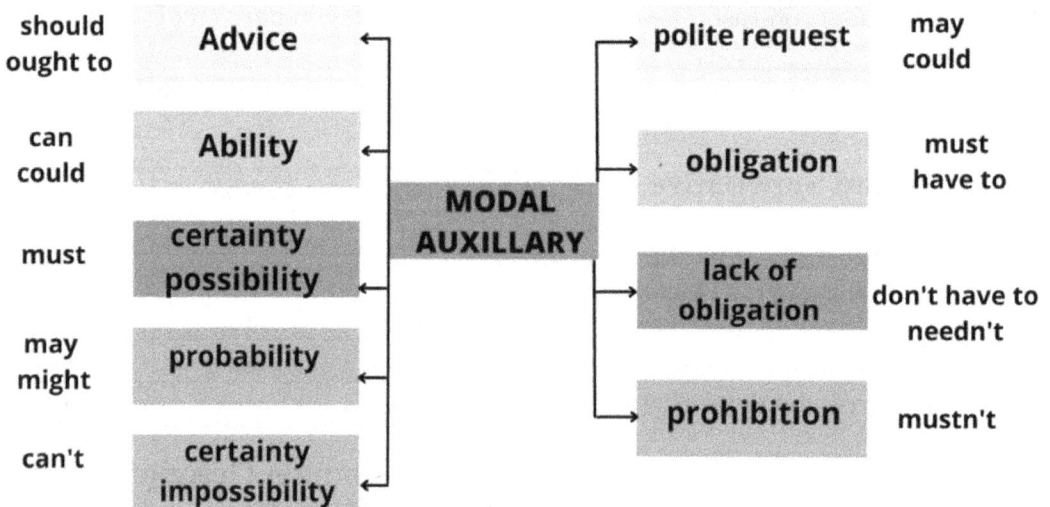

should ought to	Advice	→	polite request	may could
can could	Ability		obligation	must have to
must	certainty possibility	MODAL AUXILLARY	lack of obligation	don't have to needn't
may might	probability		prohibition	mustn't
can't	certainty impossibility			

Sensory Words Relating Touch and Taste

Words	Sentences
Chilled	She drank the **chilled** lemonade on the **hot** summer day.
Creamy	The fruit custard was **creamy** and **delicious**.
Feathery	The coat was **feathery** and **warm**.
Bumpy	The shortcut was a bad idea it gave a **bumpy** road
Chilly	The climate gets **chilly** after the evening.
Creepy	The haunted street looks **creepy**.
Fluffy	My new dog is so **fluffy** just like candy floss.
Silky	Her hair is long and **silky**.
Soft	I felt a **soft** breeze on my skin.
Warm	His new sweatshirt was **warm** and **soft** .
Tickling	She **tickled** my feet with a soft feather.
Sticky	The fresh paint was still **sticky**.
Prickly	The old mattress was hard and **prickly**.

Basic Parts of a Letter

While drafting a letter, the following points must be followed:

- **Sender's Address:** A letter must begin with sender's address. It will inform the receiver of the letter which will enable him to send the reply if he feels so.
- **Receiver's Address:** Without the address of the receiver the letter cannot reach the destination. It also tells about the person for whom the letter is meant.
- **Date:** Date is also an important point so, date must be specified.
- **Subject:** After date, subject must be specified.
- **Salutation or Greeting:** The words used for Salutation or Greeting. It depends on the person the letter is addressed to.
- **Main Body:** The message or information to be conveyed is written here.
- **Subscription:** Letter must be ended with a polite leave taking such as yours truly, yours sincerely, yours affectionately etc.
- **Signature:** The name of the sender is written at the end.

Subjective Question

1. Find the verbs in the sentences.
   (a) He tries every time.
   (b) My father drinks a lot.
   (c) We have planned the tour.
   (d) Jump into the pond.
   (e) Let Karan take the final decision.
   (f) She wants a tall husband.
   (g) We all crossed the first step.
   (h) Why do they ask me about it?
   (i) My mother always encourages me.
   (k) You broke my heart.

   Answers:
   (a) He **tries** every time.
   (b) My father **drinks** a lot.
   (c) We have **planned** the tour.
   (d) **Jump** into the pond.
   (e) **Let** Karan take the final decision.
   (f) She **wants** a tall husband.
   (g) We all **crossed** the first step.
   (h) Why do they **ask** me about it?
   (i) My mother always **encourages** me.
   (j) You **broke** my heart.

2. Choose the correct adjectives.
   (a) The _____ man was shouting at all the people. (gentle/angry/handsome)
   (b) Anushka will wear _____ boots. (sad/jealous/long)
   (c) Ruchi is the _____ girl in our family. (fancy/plane/prettiest)
   (d) These crows always fly over this _____ lake. (yellow/new/snowy)
   (e) The Taj Mahal is a _____ building in India. (newest/historical/brave)
   (f) The shoes were so _____ that I did not hesitate to buy them. (good/a lot of/tall)
   (g) My daughter wants to become a _____ girl. (tasty/successful/defeated)
   (h) The month of February has _____ number of days. (lazy/many/less)
   (i) My _____ grandfather can run yet. (old/hot/massive)
   (j) She has _____ hair. (cool/skinny/shiny)

   Answers:
   (a) The **angry** man was shouting at all the people.
   (b) Anushka will wear **long** boots.
   (c) Ruchi is the **prettiest** girl in our family.
   (d) These crows always fly over this **snowy** lake.
   (e) The Taj Mahal is a **historical** building in India.
   (f) The shoes were so **good** that I wouldn't hesitate to buy them.
   (g) My daughter wants to become a **successful** girl.
   (h) The month of February has **less** number of days.
   (i) My **old** grandfather can run yet.
   (j) She has **shiny** hair.

3. Use the correct articles (a, an, the) in the given sentences.
   (a) Shalini ma'am is _____ best teacher.
   (b) There is _____ thief in his house.

(c) Green light shows _____ signal.

(d) _____ honest person never does dishonesty.

(e) Iron is _____ heavy metal.

(f) He married _____ widow.

(g) She wanted to become _____ engineer.

(h) They live in _____ United States.

(i) The doctor suggested _____ X-ray.

(j) How much will _____ movie ticket cost?

Answers:

(a) Shalini ma'am is **the** best teacher.

(b) There is **a** thief in his house.

(c) Green light shows **a** signal.

(d) An honest person never does dishonesty.

(e) Iron is **a** heavy metal.

(f) He married **a** widow.

(g) She wanted to become **an** engineer.

(h) They live in **the** United States.

(i) The doctor suggested **an** X-ray.

(j) How much will **a** movie ticket cost?

4. Choose the correct helping verb for the given sentences.

(a) She _____ like to eat bananas. (isn't/doesn't/don't)

(b) Saumya _____ a nice mother. (is/are/am)

(c) The cow _____ given two liters of milk today. (have/had/has)

(d) Both _____ going to the restaurant. (is/are/am)

(e) Neha and Toni _____ planning for the next step. (does/are/is)

(f) We all _____ be responsible for it. (might/should/may)

(g) Atul and I _____ worried about the exams. (have/is/were)

(h) They _____ wasting their time. (have/are/will)

(i) I _____ stop him from entering the studio. (can/have/is)

(j) You _____ do better (have/can/are)

Answers:

(a) She **doesn't** like to eat bananas.

(b) Saumya **is** a nice mother.

(c) The cow **has** given two liters of milk today.

(d) Both **are** going to the restaurant.

(e) Neha and Toni **are** planning for the next step.

(f) We all **should** be responsible for it.

(g) Atul and I **were** worried about the exams.

(h) They **are** wasting their time.

(i) I **can** stop him from entering the studio.

(j) You **are** doing better.

5. Use the correct preposition in the sentences.

(a) My mother packed four loaves of bread _____ the lunch box.

(b) Noah wakes up _____ 6 o'clock every day.

(c) He comes _____ me _____ the evening.

(d) She bought a woolen t-shirt _____ her father.

(e) This bike was gifted _____ my sister.

(f) Would you sing _____ me?

(g) Vishal has been suffering _____ dengue.

(h) Add three cups _____ sugar.

(i) There happened a fight _____ Shobhit and Harsh.

(j) He slapped Ekta _____ me.

Answers:

(a) My mother packed four loaves of bread **in** the lunch box.

(b) Noah wakes up **at** 6 o'clock every day.

(c) He comes **to** me **in** the evening.

(d) She bought a woolen t-shirt **for** her father.

(e) This bike was gifted **by** my sister.

(f) Would you sing **with** me?

(g) Vishal has been suffering **from** dengue.

(h) Add three cups **of** sugar.

(i) There happened a fight **between** Shobhit and Harsh.

(j) He slapped Ekta **in front of** me.

6. Convert the given sentences to the present continuous tense.

(a) I do yoga at home

(b) She watches cartoons.

(c) They play chess with family members.

(d) Mona likes to talk with strangers.

(e) You sit under the tree

(f) The hen eats insects.

(g) He takes interest in me.

(h) We go to London.

(i) You put this on the table.

(j) The sun rises.

Answers:

(a) I **am doing** yoga at home

(b) She **is watching** cartoons.

(c) They **are playing** chess with family members.

(d) Mona **likes** talking to with strangers.

(e) You **are sitting** under the tree

(f) The hen **is eating** insects.

(g) He **is taking** interest in me.

(h) We **are going** to London.

(i) You **are putting** this on the table.

(j) The sun **is rising**.

7. Match the opposite words.

Active	Free
Excited	New
Clever	Separate
Old	Bottom
Arrest	Niece
Gallant	Cloudy
Together	Lazy
Nephew	Foolish
Top	Cowardly
Sunny	Calm

Answers:

Word	Opposite word
Active	Lazy
Excited	Calm
Clever	Foolish
Old	New
Arrest	Free
Gallant	Cowardly
Together	Separate
Nephew	Niece
Top	Bottom
Sunny	Cloudy

8. Find the kind of noun the underline word has.

(a) She had <u>pain</u> in her legs.

Answer: An abstract noun is the name of some state, quality, feeling or idea that we can only think of or feel but cannot touch or See. Therefore, pain is an abstract noun.

(b) Most of the <u>doctors</u> in our country avoid to serve in rural areas.

Answer: A Common Noun is the name given to the class of person. Therefore, doctor is a common noun.

(c) Elephants more often move in <u>herd</u>.

Answer: A Collective Noun is the name of a group or collection. Therefore, herd is a collective noun

(d) Students sit together in the class.

Answer: A Common Noun is common for a group. Therefore, students is a common noun.

(e) New York is a beautiful city.

Answer: A Proper Noun is the name of a particular place. Therefore, New York is a proper noun.

(f) The man is known for his wisdom.

Answer: An Abstract Noun is the name of some state, quality, feeling or idea that we can only think of or feel but cannot touch or See. Therefore, wisdom is an abstract noun.

(g) The commercial capital of India is Mumbai.

Answer: A Proper Noun is the name of a particular city. Therefore, Mumbai is a proper noun.

9. Fill in the blanks with a correct kind of noun from the following options:

(a) A _____ of shoes.

Answer: A pair of shoes (Collective Noun). A Collective Noun is the name of a group or collection of person things or animals. So, A pair of shoes is a group of shoes.

(b) A _____ of players.

Answer: A team of players (Collective Noun). A Collective Noun is the name of a group or collection of person things or animals. So, A team of players is a group of players.

(c) The _____ of this room is four meters.

Answer: Length. An abstract noun is the name of some state, quality, feeling or idea that we can only think of or feel but cannot touch or See.

10. Choose the kind of pronoun the underline word has.

(a) That kind of job is really very difficult.

Answer: That is a demonstrative pronoun.

(b) Those people were really brilliant.

Answer: Those is a demonstrative pronoun.

(c) Who are you to interfere in this matter?

Answer: In this sentence, the pronoun who is used to ask a question. Therefore, who is an interrogative pronoun

(d) Anyone called me?

Answer: In this sentence, the pronoun anyone refers to something that is not definite. Therefore, anyone is an indefinite pronoun.

(e) He learns himself.

Answer: In this sentence, the pronoun himself is used as object of the verb where the subject and object are the same person or thing. Therefore, himself is a reflexive pronoun.

11. Correct the order of words below to form meaningful sentence.

(a) Doctor / is a / my / father

Answer: The correct sentence is, "My father is a doctor".

(b) The peacock / India / of / is / bird / the national.

Answer: The correct sentence is, "The peacock is the national bird of India".

(c) Flowers / everywhere / there / are / the spring / during.

Answer: During the spring, "There are flowers everywhere".

(d) Lights / festival / of / the / Diwali / is.

Answer: The correct answer is, "Diwali is the festival of lights".

(e) Land / of / India / farmers / is a.
Answer: The correct answer is, "India is a land of farmers".

12. Fill in the blanks with suitable Conjunction.

(a) We told you _____ he would not play.
Answer: We told you that he would not play.

(b) She tried hard _____ failed.
Answer: She tried hard but failed

(c) Rozy won the prize _____ her parents were happy.
Answer: Rozy won the prize so her parents were happy.

(d) He is injured _____ he cannot run
Answer: He is injured so he cannot run.

(e) He was punished _____ he was not guilty.
Answer: He was punished though he was not guilty.

13. See the Picture and answer the questions that follows.

1. Where are the children playing?
Answer: The children are playing in the park.

2. How many children are playing?
Answer: Six children are playing.

3. How many children are reading?
Answer: One child is reading a book with her grandmother.

4. What activities are happening in the picture?
Answer: The picture is of a park where an old lady is sitting with a girl, and both of them are reading a book. There is a boy behind the bench who is probably trying to hide. The two children are climbing up the tree. There is a girl who is riding her bike and a boy with a pet is running behind her.

14. Read the following unseen passage mindfully and answer the questions given below.

Smile is the best tonic for our mind and body. It takes thirteen muscles to smile, but forty-three to be angry. So, it is easier to smile and difficult to be angry. To be cheerful, we have to create positive thoughts. On the other hand, if we constantly think about negative things, we feel unhappy. So, the best way to avoid a negative idea is to replace it with a positive one. When we are relaxed in bed, we should practise putting some cheerful thoughts.

1. What is the best tonic for our mind and body?
2. What should we do to be cheerful?
3. What is the best way to replace a negative idea?
4. What should we practise when we are relaxed in bed?

5. What happens when we constantly think about negative things?

Answers:

1: Smile is the best tonic for our mind and body.

2: To be cheerful, we have to create positive thoughts.

3: The best way to avoid a negative idea is to replace it with a positive one.

4: When we are relaxed in bed, we should practise putting some cheerful thoughts.

5: When we constantly think about negative things, we feel unhappy.

15. Read the following unseen passage mindfully and answer the questions given below.

The Sun is a star around which many planets revolve such as Mercury, Venus, Earth, Mars, Jupiter, etc. The nearest planet to the Sun is Mercury and Neptune is the farthest one. There are total of eight planets in the solar system.

The sun is a ball made of gases like helium, carbon, and hydrogen but it has the largest amount of helium and hydrogen gas. The temperature of the outer surface of the Sun is about 5500°C, which is very high.

Also, there are some such stars that are bigger and brighter than the Sun in the entire galaxy.

The Sun plays an important role in eclipses. A solar eclipse occurs when the Moon comes between the Sun and the Earth whereas, a lunar eclipse occurs when the Earth comes between the Sun and the Moon.

Questions:

1. Write the names of any three planets.
2. Which planet is the nearest to the Sun?
3. What is the temperature of the outer surface of the Sun?
4. When does a solar eclipse occur?
5. How many planets are there in the solar system?

Answers:

1. Earth, Mars, Jupiter.
2. The nearest planet to the sun is Mercury.
3. The temperature of the outer surface of the Sun is about 5500°C.
4. A solar eclipse occurs when the Moon comes between the Sun and the Earth.
5. There are a total of eight planets in the solar system.

Model Test Paper

SECTION I: Word and Structure Knowledge

Direction (1–5): Choose the correct antonym.

1. Descend
   - (a) Fly
   - (b) Down
   - (c) Ascend
   - (d) Side

2. Grow
   - (a) Shrink
   - (b) Hope
   - (c) Fast
   - (d) Lean

3. Hate
   - (a) Loyal
   - (b) Love
   - (c) Joy
   - (d) Like

4. Foolish
   - (a) Wisdom
   - (b) Intelligent
   - (c) Simple
   - (d) Wise

5. Loose
   - (a) Tight
   - (b) Phase
   - (c) Big
   - (d) Fit

Direction (6–10): Choose the correct synonym.

6. Oral
   - (a) Colour
   - (b) Teeth
   - (c) Mouth
   - (d) Verbal

7. Blank
   - (a) Paper
   - (b) Empty
   - (c) Thin
   - (d) Full

8. Glad
   - (a) Cheerful
   - (b) Gloomy
   - (c) Happy
   - (d) Depressed

9. Clever
   - (a) Impertinent
   - (b) Dumb
   - (c) Intelligent
   - (d) Sly

10. Quick
    - (a) Fast
    - (b) Ink
    - (c) Set
    - (d) Slow

Direction (11–15): Fill in the blanks.

11. He completed this sum_____ his classmate
    - (a) At
    - (b) For
    - (c) On
    - (d) To

12. He came home _____school.
    - (a) Into
    - (b) On
    - (c) From
    - (d) To

13. Go_____the garden.
    - (a) Into
    - (b) To
    - (c) For
    - (d) From

14. He sent me a box____books.
    - (a) Of
    - (b) On
    - (c) To
    - (d) Up

15. He sat_____the tree.
    - (a) On
    - (b) In
    - (c) Under
    - (d) At

Directions (16–20): Form a meaningful word from the given spellings.

16. Dernow
    - (a) Derwon
    - (b) Rednow
    - (c) Nowder
    - (d) Wonder

17. Ganibar
    - (a) Anigrab
    - (b) Bargain
    - (c) Ingarab
    - (d) Baragin

18. Porulap
    - (a) Ruoplap
    - (b) Ulapurop
    - (c) Popular
    - (d) Larupop

19. Veerg
    - (a) Verge
    - (b) Geerv
    - (c) Egerv
    - (d) Veger

20. Flatret
    - (a) Afltret
    - (b) Flatter
    - (c) Fletatr
    - (d) Letfrat

SECTION II: Reading

Everyday, we see the breadman coming faithfully on his scooter to deliver bread to our homes. He is regular and brings fresh from the bakery, loaves of bread, cakes, biscuits and buns to all those who have placed orders for these items.

He has loaves of bread hanging in plastic bags on either side of his scooter, along with other items wrapped up in packets too. Sometimes, dogs chase him and bark at him, but he just carries on with his delivery and they soon leave him alone as they get used to his appearance each day. Occasionally, he throws a bun or a biscuit to the dog and this helps to keep it quiet. Thunder storms drive most people indoors, yet the breadman braves the bad weather and calls on us regularly. He wears a raincoat to protect himself from the rain and, on hot days, his helmet shades him from the scorching sun. He is helpful and reliable and does his bit for the community. We appreciate his services.

Answer the following questions based on passage given.

21. The breadman comes _____.
    (a) Twice a day   (b) Daily
    (c) Bi-monthly   (d) Weekly

22. How is the breadman described?
    (a) Unfortunate and unlucky
    (b) lazy and sly
    (c) incompetent and rude
    (d) industrious and reliable

23. The breadman only delivers bread.
    (a) True   (b) False
    (c) Unclear

24. The breadman is kind only to human beings.
    (a) True   (b) False
    (c) Unclear

25. Community means:
    (a) group of people inhabiting the same locality
    (b) To communicate to a unit
    (c) To commune from very far
    (d) To form unity

The modern pizza was originally invented in Naples, Italy but the word pizza is Greek in origin, derived from the Greek word *pektos* meaning *solid* or *clotted*. The ancient Greeks covered their bread with oils, herbs and cheese. The first major innovation that led to flat bread pizza was the use of tomato as a topping. It was common for the poor of the area around Naples to add tomato to their yeast-based flat bread, and so the pizza began. While it is difficult to say for sure who invented the pizza, it is, however, believed that modern pizza was first made by baker Raffaele Esposito of Naples. In fact, a popular urban legend holds that the archetypal pizza, Pizza Margherita, was invented in 1889, when the Royal Palace of Capodimonte commissioned the Neapolitan pizzaiolo Raffaele Esposito to create a pizza in honour of the visiting Queen Margherita. Of the three different pizzas he created, the Queen strongly preferred a pie swathed in the colours of the Italian flag: red (tomato), green (basil), and white (mozzarella). Supposedly, this kind of pizza was then named after the Queen as Pizza Margherita.

Answer the following questions based on passage given.

26. Where is Naples?
    (a) Germany   (b) Greece
    (c) Spain   (d) Italy

27. Innovation means inventing something new.
    (a) True   (b) False
    (c) Wrong info   (d) None

28. Historians know who invented the pizza.
    (a) True   (b) False

29. The word 'Pizza' is Italian in origin.
    (a) True   (b) False

30. A ' pizzaiolo' is a Pizza maker.
    (a) True   (b) False

SECTION III: Spoken And Written Expression
Choose the correct option.

31. Teacher: Everyone, hand in your papers.
    Student:
    (a) Ma'am don't be mean
    (b) Yes ma'am
    (c) One more minute
    (d) No

32. Lily: It's a hot day.

James:

(a) It could be worse.

(b) Yes

(c) It's terrible.

(d) Why did you drag me out?

33. James: It's so difficult to exercise.

Nicky:

(a) Let's stop.

(b) That's because you're lazy.

(c) So?

(d) Yes, but it is invigorating.

34. Priti: I'm so tired.

Shalmi:

(a) Me too.

(b) Hmmm.

(c) Why don't you rest?

(d) I don't care.

35. Luke: Do your best !

Sally:

(a) I think I won't.

(b) Thank you, I'll try.

(c) I am very sleepy.

(d) I don't want to.

🕐🕐🕐

Model Test Paper

2

SECTION I: Word And Structure Knowledge

Direction (1–5): Choose the correct antonyms

1. Polite
   (a) Rude   (b) Happy
   (c) Manners   (d) Avoid

2. Permanent
   (a) Same   (b) Always
   (c) Transient (d) Temporary

3. Virtue
   (a) Evil   (b) Bad
   (c) Vice   (d) Less

4. Straight
   (a) Circle   (b) Crooked
   (c) Line   (d) Narrow

5. Success
   (a) Lose   (b) Failure
   (c) Immense   (d) Fail

Direction (6–10): Choose the correct synonyms.

6. Eatable
   (a) Edible   (b) Oral
   (c) Tasty   (d) Poisonous

7. Indolent
   (a) Calm   (b) Industrious
   (c) Furious   (d) Lazy

8. Feeble
   (a) Unable   (b) Alert
   (c) Weak   (d) Secure

9. Scarce
   (a) Usual   (b) Rare
   (c) Plenty   (d) Unavailable

10. Real
    (a) Genuine (b) Ready
    (c) Lean   (d) Fake

Direction (11–15): Fill in the blanks with correct prepositions.

11. A lamp was hung _____ my head.
    (a) At   (b) Over
    (c) Above   (d) On

12. He sailed_____the sea.
    (a) Across   (b) Through
    (c) On   (d) To

13. He returned_____many days.
    (a) For   (b) After
    (c) From   (d) Into

14. He is not_____home just now.
    (a) At   (b) On
    (c) To   (d) For

15. I will tell him ____ call you.
    (a) On   (b) For
    (c) At   (d) To

Directions (16–20): Make a meaningful word.

16. Glaryoss
    (a) Ossalgry (b) lossgary
    (c) sarsyolg (d) Glossary

17. Micag
    (a) Lmcag   (b) Magic
    (c) Cagmi   (d) Migac

18. Copomse
    (a) Compose   (b) Seomcop
    (c) Ompocse   (d) Seocmop

19. Flerify
    (a) Elfrify   (b) Fleriyf
    (c) Firefly   (d) Flyfire

20. Matecil
    (a) Cetamli   (b) Climate
    (c) limatec   (d) Mliatec

SECTION II: Reading

Pollution is the degradation of natural environment by the introduction of external substances directly or indirectly into natural resources such as air and water. Human health, ecosystem and aquatic and terrestrial biodiversity may be affected and altered permanently due to pollution. Pollution occurs when ecosystems cannot get rid of substances introduced into the environment. The critical threshold of its ability to naturally eliminate substances is compromised and the balance of the ecosystem is broken.

The sources and reasons of pollution are numerous. The identification of these different pollutants and their effects on ecosystems is complex. They can come from natural disasters or the result of human activity such as oil spills, chemical spills, nuclear accidents etc. These can have terrible consequences on people and the planet: destruction of the biodiversity, increased mortality of the human and animal species, destruction of natural habitat, damage caused to the quality of soil, water and air.

Preventing pollution and protecting the environment necessitate the application of the principles of sustainable development. We have to consider the needs of today without compromising the ability of future generations to meet their needs. This means that we should remedy existing pollution, but also anticipate and prevent future pollution sources in order to protect the environment and public health. Any environmental damage must be punishable by law, and polluters should pay compensation for the damage caused to the environment.

Answer the following questions based on passage given.

21. The degradation of natural environment by external substances introduced directly or indirectly is known as
    (a) Pollution   (b) Disastrous
    (c) Harmful   (d) Polluters

22. Pollution only has a temporary effect
    (a) True   (b) False

23. Only the aquatic and terrestrial ecosystems are disturbed.
    (a) True   (b) False

24. The ecosystem can always cope with pollutants.
    (a) False   (b) True

25. Pollution is caused by
    (a) Aliens
    (b) Natural disasters
    (c) Both b and d
    (d) Human activity

Mickey Mouse is a cartoon character who has become an icon for the Walt Disney Company. Mickey Mouse is short for Mitchell Mouse. It was created in 1928 by **Walt Disney** and **Ub Iwerks** and voiced by **Walt Disney**. The first appearance of Mickey Mouse was in *Plane Crazy* on May 15, 1928. But the Walt Disney Company celebrates Mickey Mouse birthday on November 18, 1928 upon the release of *Steamboat Willie*, because it is the first Mickey Mouse Cartoon with sound. The anthropomorphic mouse has developed along the years. He first appeared in colour in 1935. The first **Technicolor Disney** film was **Flowers and Trees** in 1932. He also evolved from being simply a character in animated cartoons and comic strips to become one of the most recognizable symbols in the world. Popularity has grown around the world. This was due to his angelic nature. Mickey never does anything immoral. However, in 2009 the Walt Disney Company announced that they will begin to re-brand the Mickey Mouse character by moving away from his pleasant, cheerful image and reintroducing the more devious side of his personality, starting with the upcoming **Epic Mickey,** a Mickey Mouse video game. The Walt Disney Company thus intends to show the mischievous side of Mickey's personality.

Answer the following questions based on passage given.

26. When is Mickey Mouse's birthday?
    (a) May 18, 1932
    (b) November 18, 1928
    (c) November 15, 1935
    (d) May 15, 1928

27. The first Mickey Mouse with sound appeared in 'Steamboat Willie'.
    (a) True   (b) False

28. The first Technicolour film was 'Steamboat Willie'.
    (a) False   (b) True

29. Animated means
    (a) Funny jokes
    (b) Full of life
    (c) Made using animation techniques
    (d) Animal related

30. What is 'Epic Mickey'?
    (a) Comic book   (b) Movie
    (c) Comic strip   (d) A video game

SECTION III: Spoken and Written Expression

Choose the correct option.

31. Malini: Would you please call your mother?
    Chinki:
    (a) Yes, just wait a minute.
    (b) Maybe, if you give me a chocolate.
    (c) I don't feel like it.
    (d) No.

32. Tony: We never see you these days.
    Mack:
    (a) I forgot about you all.
    (b) I had some work.
    (c) Sorry, I have been out of town.
    (d) Why are you bothering me?

33. Boss: Try to get the deal signed by today.
    Secretary:
    (a) You should do it since you're the Boss.
    (b) You do it.
    (c) I'll do my best.
    (d) I can't.

34. Reggie: I got the highest marks in class!
    Betty:
    (a) I wanted to get the highest.
    (b) Congratulations!
    (c) You didn't deserve them.
    (d) Who cares?

35. Uncle: How are you?
    Rima:
    (a) Do you really care?
    (b) You don't need to know.
    (c) Fine.
    (d) Good, how are you?

🕐🕐🕐

Answer Keys

SECTION 1: WORD AND STRUCTURE KNOWLEDGE

1. SPELLINGS AND COLLOCATIONS

Answer Key				
I				
1. Priest	2. Queen	3. Boxes	4. Misinformed	5. Driving
6. Almost	7. Thief	8. Supplied	9. Played	10. Unaware
11. Also	12. Writing	13. Quickly	14. Unwashed	15. Briefcase
16. Stayed	17. Multiplied	18. Giving	19. Almost	20. Carried
21. Foxes	22. Piece	23. Keeping	24. Unsure	25. Typed
26. Quack	27. Unwashed	28. Relaxes	29. Niece	30. Also
II				
1. Take	2. Making	3. Waste	4. Bitterly	5. Falling
6. Litter	7. Fluent	8. Rich	9. Heavy	10. Strong
11. Warm	12. Record	13. Works	14. Permission	15. Threw
16. Feel	17. Red handed	18. Spirit	19. Wish	20. Maintenance
III				
1. Free	2. Temperatures	3. Money	4. Lost	5. Flies
6. Joy	7. Cake	8. Roar	9. Mind	10. Stupid

HOTS

I
1. Do you like Marathi food?
2. What is your roll number?
3. Will you be able to pick the things up today?
4. How often do you call granny?
5. Is it safe to drive at night on a highway?

II				
1. in	2. on	3. in	4. across	5. in
6. on	7. by, by	8. by	9. at	10. you

2. ANIMALS, HOUSING AND FOOD

Answer Key

I				
1. Stationery	2. Cutlery	3. Spices	4. Clothes	5. Toiletries
6. Utensils	7. Spices	8. Stationery	9. Clothes	10. Spices
11. Toiletries	12. Utensils	13. Vehicles	14. Stationery	15. Decorative items

II				
1. Prayer room	2. Garage	3. Study room	4. Drawing room	5. Gym
6. Terrace	7. Bathroom	8. Drawing room	9. Kitchen	10. Study room
11. Bathroom	12. Prayer room	13. Garage	14. Drawing room	15. Bedroom

III		
1. Packaged or cooked food	2. Grains	3. Fruits
4. Packaged cooked food	5. Processed fruits and vegetables	6. Grains
7. Vegetables	8. Packaged cooked food	9. Vegetables
10. Fruits		

IV		
1. Women's casual	2. Men's formal	3. Women's formal
4. Children	5. Women's casual	6. Women's formal
7. Sports	8. Men's formal	9. Women's casual
10. Men's casual		

HOTS

1. Dogs, sheep, horses, cows, chicken
2. Sqrirrels, cows, dogs, pigeons, goats
3. Wild cats, camels, lizards, eagles, foxes
4. Black buck, hog-deer, elephants, rhinoceros,

3. EMOTIONS

Answer Key

1. Love	2. Anger	3. Fear	4. Love	5. Shame
6. Anger	7. Sadness	8. Surprise	9. Fear	10. Love
11. Anger	12. Sadness	13. Surprise	14. Shame	15. Fear

HOTS

1. Sadness	2. Happiness	3. Shame	4. Envy	5. Fear
6. Anger	7. Love	8. Surprise	9. Sadness	10. Shame
11. Anger	12. Happiness	13. Fear	14. Love	15. Shame

4. SYNONYMS AND ANTONYMS

Answer Key									
I									
1. (a)	2. (a)	3. (d)	4. (c)	5. (d)	6. (d)	7. (b)	8. (a)	9. (d)	10. (d)
11. (b)	12. (a)	13. (c)	14. (a)	15. (c)	16. (c)	17. (a)	18. (a)	19. (b)	20. (a)
II									
1. (a)	2. (a)	3. (d)	4. (d)	5. (a)	6. (a)	7. (d)	8. (b)	9. (d)	10. (d)
11. (c)	12. (a)	13. (d)	14. (d)	15. (a)	16. (b)	17. (d)	18. (b)	19. (c)	20. (b)

HOTS				
1. (c)	2. (a)	3. (a)	4. (b)	5. (a)

5. NOUNS

Answer Key									
I									
1. (a)	2. (c)	3. (d)	4. (b)	5. (c)	6. (d)	7. (c)	8. (c)	9. (d)	10. (a)
11. (a)	12. (c)	13. (b)	14. (b)	15. (a)	16. (b)	17. (d)	18. (c)	19. (d)	20. (d)

HOTS				
1. (d)	2. (c)	3. (c)	4. (d)	5. (b)

6. PRONOUNS

Answer Key									
I									
1. (d)	2. (c)	3. (b)	4. (d)	5. (a)	6. (d)	7. (a)	8. (b)	9. (d)	10. (a)
11. (b)	12. (c)	13. (b)	14. (c)	15. (a)					
II									
1. (b)	2. (d)	3. (a)	4. (c)	5. (d)	6. (a)	7. (c)	8. (b)	9. (a)	10. (b)
11. (d)	12. (a)	13. (b)	14. (c)	15. (b)					

HOTS				
1. (b)	2. (c)	3. (b)	4. (c)	5. (d)

1. (b) as you and him are representing people.
2. (c) as ours show possession.
3. (b) as we, us, it represent people or things.
4. (c) as theirs show possession
5. (d) as myself represents going back to itself.

7. VERBS

Answer Key				
I				
1. Sung	2. Cost	3. Won	4. Seen	5. Flew
6. Became	7. Cut	8. Written	9. Built	10. Chosen
11. Gave, saw	12. Spent	13. Understood	14. Taken	15. Knew
II				
1. Showed	2. Eaten	3. Shrunk	4. Chose	5. Gone
6. Costs	7. Met	8. Heard	9. Torn	10. Caught
11. Threw	12. Showed	13. Drawn	14. Made	15. Came

8. MODALS

Answer Key

I

1. Will	2. Should	3. Would	4. May	5. Might
6. Can	7. May	8. May	9. Will	10. Would
11. Could	12. Should	13. Shall	14. Will	15. Would
16. Would	17. Can	18. Shall	19. Might	20. Would

II

1. May	2. Would	3. Will	4. Can	5. Shall
6. May	7. Might	8. May	9. Will	10. Would

HOTS				
1. (b)	2. (d)	3. (a)	4. (c)	5. (a)

1. (b) Option (b) fits in correctly as it reports the action completed by the dancer. Option (a) could have also been applicable, but it cannot be so because its first letter is capital. That renders only option (b) as correct.

2. (d) Option (d) only becomes applicable with reference to the word yesterday.

3. (a) Option (a) only is applicable. In option (b), the word begins with a capital letter and thus cannot be used in the middle of that sentence which renders it incorrect.

4. (c) Terrorists attacked WTC by hijacking aeroplanes.

9. ADVERBS

Answer Key				
I.				
1. Degree	2. Cause and effect	3. Manner	4. Place	5. Place
6. Manner	7. Manner	8. Number	9. Number	10. Relative
11. Degree	12. Time	13. Condition (interrgative)	14. Degree	15. Time
16. Number	17. Manner	18. Time	19. Degree	20. Time
II.				
1. When	2. How	3. How much	4. Where	5. When
6. How	7. Where	8. When	9. How many	10. How many

HOTS				
1. At 11	2. Assam	3. Partially agree	4. Crunchy	5. Therefore

10. ADJECTIVES

Answer Key									
1. (b)	2. (b)	3. (a)	4. (b)	5. (a)	6. (b)	7. (a)	8. (a)	9. (a)	10. (b)
11. (b)	12. (b)	13. (a)	14. (b)	15. (a)	16. (a)	17. (a)	18. (a)	19. (b)	20. (b)

HOTS				
1. (a)	2. (a)	3. (a)	4. (c)	5. (c)

11. CONTRACTIONS

HOTS

1. (b)	2. (b)	3. (a)	4. (c)	5. (d)

12. ARTICLES

HOTS

Once upon a time, there lived an ant and a grasshopper in a grassy meadow. It was during the hot summer season when the ant was toiling hard by collecting wheat grains from the farmer's field. On the other hand, the grasshopper spent all his time in singing and dancing. He would frequently call the ant to join him in singing and dancing. However, the ant would ignore him and continue with her work. The ant said that she was saving some food for the cold season and recommended the grasshopper to follow the same. The grasshopper didn't pay heed to her words and continued singing and dancing merrily. Soon summer faded to autumn and autumn to winter. Out of cold, the grasshopper lost his interest in singing and making merry. He was cold and hungry and had no place to take shelter from the snow outside. Suddenly he remembered about the ant and visited her for some food and shelter. The grasshopper made an approach to her for some food and shelter. She gently asked him to sing somewhere else and earn his food and shelter. It is then, the grasshopper realized that he should have saved up enough for the winter instead of wasting his time being lazy during summer in singing and dancing around.

13. PREPOSITIONS

Answer Key									
I.									
1. On	2. In	3. On	4. On	5. In	6. In	7. At	8. In	9. On	10. At
II.									
1. On	2. In	3. At	4. In	5. In	6. At	7. On	8. In	9. On/In	10. At
III.									
1. Incorrect/in		2. Correct		3. Correct		4. Incorrect/in		5. Incorrect/by	
6. Correct		7. Correct		8. Incorrect/in		9. Incorrect/at		10. Correct	

HOTS

I. Gautam Buddha was born in 563 BC at Lumbini in Sakya Kshatriya clan of Kapilvastu on Vaiskha Purnima Day. His father Suddhodhana was the Saka ruler, his mother Mahamaya died after 7 days of his birth, so he was brought up by stepmother Gautami. He left home at the age of 29 years. He attained enlightenment at 35 years of age at Bodh Gaya under a pipal tree on the banks of Phalgu river on the 49th day of meditation.

II. (1) The government of India has decided to celebrate the birthday of Netaji Subhash Chandra Bose, on 23rd January, as 'Parakram Diwas' every year. This day will be dedicated to honour and remember Netaji's selfless service to the nation.

(2) I love to keep my room neat and clean. My books and other study materials are on my table. My t-shirts are in the cupboard. The shoes of mine are in the shoe rack. There is a ceiling fan above my bed. I have a TV on the wall of the room. There is a big photograph of my parents beside the TV.

(3) A greedy dog wandered in search for food. He stood near a meat shop. He stole a large piece of meat and ran away with it. He found a river on his way. There was a bridge over it. When he was crossing the bridge, he saw his own reflection in the water. He thought that it was another dog. He wanted that piece of meat also. So he barked at his own reflection. He opened his mouth and the piece of meat fell into the water. Then he repented for his action.

III. (b)

14. CONJUNCTIONS

				Answer Key					
1. (d)	2. (b)	3. (a)	4. (c)	5. (d)	6. (a)	7. (b)	8. (b)	9. (b)	10. (a)
11. (b)	12. (a)	13. (c)	14. (a)	15. (b)	16. (b)	17. (c)	18. (d)	19. (a)	20. (d)

	HOTS			
1. (c)	2. (d)	3. (d)	4. (a)	5. (b)

15. TENSES

Answer Key				
I.				
1. Opens	2. Will call	3. Will spill over	4. Talked	5. Swim
6. Is	7. Says	8. Will take us	9. Is going to speak	10. Heated
11. Comes	12. Sailed	13. Will get	14. Am going to	15. Rings

				II.					
1. (a)	2. (c)	3. (c)	4. (d)	5. (b)	6. (a)	7. (b)	8. (c)	9. (a)	10. (b)
11. (d)	12. (d)	13. (c)	14. (a)	15. (b)					

HOTS				
1. evaporates	2. gets	3. goes	4. condenses	5. go
6. comes	7. do you know	8. happens	9. does not seep	10. collects
11. rises	12. converts			

16. JUMBLED WORDS AND PUNCTUATIONS

Answer Key									
1. (b)	2. (a)	3. (c)	4. (b)	5. (c)	6. (a)	7. (b)	8. (a)	9. (a)	10. (c)
11. (c)	12. (a)	13. (c)	14. (b)	15. (a)					

HOTS				
1. (a)	2. (c)	3. (b)	4. (d)	5. (b)

SECTION 2: READING COMPREHENSION

TIPS ON READING COMPREHENSION

Answer Key
Comprehension 1
1. (a) Very joyful and content.
(b) Being completely different from each other.
(c) To be unhappy because someone has something that you want for yourself.
(d) You have to bear the consequences of your actions.
(e) To be healthy, strong and fit.
2. (a) Anand worked at a sugar factory.
(b) Yes, he liked working there because he liked eating sweets.
(c) No
(d) At Anand's house.
(e) Anand used to save grains for the winters.
(f) Gautam went to the king of the jungle, the lion to complain.
(g) Gautam told the king that there should be a law to ensure everybody gets food when hungry.

(h) No
(i) The king told Gautam that he can't take fruits of labour away from Anand.
(j) We should work hard to secure our future otherwise we will reap what we sow.
Comprehension 2
1. It was Revathy's birthday.
2. Anish couldn't go to Revathy's birthday party because he was busy with cricket practice.
3. Yes, the team has a good chance of in the Zonal finals.
4. For three years.
5. Yes, Gopal did go to Revathy's party.
6. The kids went paintball shooting in the afternoon.
7. The kids went to McDonald's for lunch.
8. No, Anish has never been paint balling.
9. To an outlet in sector-18.
10. For two hours.
11. Revathy and Aisha were captains of two teams respectively.
12. Revathy and has team won the paint-ball competition.
13. Little toys that come with happy meal at McDonald's.
14. Yes.
15. At the McDonald's.
16. Rohan won the first round.
17. The clown made the kids laugh a lot.
18. The magician made a rabbit disappear and showed a mile-long handkerchief.
19. The gymnasts swaying on the trapeze looked like hanging from the sky.
20. Anish and Gopal saw the highlights of the football match that was played the night before.

Comprehension 3

1. 2015	2. 107	3. One billion	4. 2011	5. 8 fours	6. Right hander	7. Two times
8. 22	9. Twice	10. Sachin Tendulker	11. Dhawan and Raina	12. 74	13. Sohail	14. 27 runs
15. 4 wickets						

Comprehension 4

1. 15th May 2014

2. To a farmhouse

3. One hour

4. Treasure Island

5. Kolkata

6. Fish

7. Because she liks to eat fish all the time.

8. That we are the famous five.

9. Because they were six in number

10. Because Sonu still gets her shoelace tied by her mom.

11. Hanging lights, floating lights and lights stuck on various things.

12. Preeti.

13. To a German man

14. Chocolate

15. To get married every year.

16. She gave poster of an old painter.

17. The name was Gogh

18. Overeating

19. Stomach ache

20. Next day

SECTION 3: SPOKEN AND WRITTEN EXPRESSIONS

TIPS FOR GOOD CONVERSATION

Answer Key

I.		
1. Introduction	2. Accepting request	3. Apology
4. Greeting	5. Accepting apology	6. Introduction
7. Accepting apology	8. Responding to requeat	9. Accepting apology
10. Greeting	11. Introduction	12. Responding to request
13. Apology	14. Greeting	15. Accepting apology

II.									
1. (a)	2. (c)	3. (b)	4. (a)	5. (b)	6. (c)	7. (a)	8. (c)	9. (b)	10. (c)

MODEL TEST PAPER – 1

Answer Key

I.									
1. (c)	2. (a)	3. (b)	4. (d)	5. (a)	6. (d)	7. (b)	8. (c)	9. (c)	10. (a)
11. (b)	12. (c)	13. (b)	14. (a)	15. (a)	16. (d)	17. (b)	18. (c)	19. (a)	20. (b)

II.									
21. (b)	22. (d)	23. (b)	24. (b)	25. (a)	26. (d)	27. (a)	28. (b)	29. (b)	30. (a)

III.									
31. (b)	32. (b)	33. (d)	34. (c)	35. (b)					

MODEL TEST PAPER – 2

Answer Key

I.

1. (a)	2. (d)	3. (c)	4. (b)	5. (b)	6. (a)	7. (d)	8. (c)	9. (b)	10. (a)
11. (b)	12. (a)	13. (b)	14. (a)	15. (d)	16. (d)	17. (b)	18. (a)	19. (c)	20. (b)

II.

21. (a)	22. (b)	23. (b)	24. (a)	25. (c)	26. (b)	27. (a)	28. (a)	29. (c)	30. (d)

III.

31 (a)	32. (c)	33. (c)	34. (b)	35. (d)					

Appendix

There are different organizations that conduct these examinations and covering all of them is not needed as the focus should be to understand the main type of exams conducted. They are similar for these organizations with the difference being the change in name of the exam.

S. No.	Science Olympiad Foundation (SOF)	
	Name of Exam	Grade
1.	National Science Olympiad (NSO)	Class 1-10
2.	National Cyber Olympiad (NCO)	Class 1-10
3.	International Mathematics Olympiad (IMO)	Class 1-10
4.	International English Olympiad (IEO)	Class 1-10
5.	International Commerce Olympiad (ICO)	Class 1-10
6.	International General Knowledge Olympiad (IGKO)	Class 1-10
7.	International Social Studies Olympiad (ISSO)	Class 1-10

S. No.	Indian Talent Olympiad (ITO)	
	Name of Exam	Grade
1.	International Science Olympiad (ISO)	Class 1-12
2.	International Math Olympiad (IMO)	Class 1-12
3.	English International Olympiad (EIO)	Class 1-12
4.	General Knowledge International Olympiad (GKIO)	Class 1-12
5.	International Computer Olympiad (ICO)	Class 1-12
6.	International Drawing Olympiad (IDO)	Class 1-12
7.	National Essay Olympiad (NESO)	Class 1-12
8.	National Social Studies Olympiad (NSSO)	Class 1-12

S. No.	EduHeal Foundation	
	Name of Exam	Grade
1.	Eduheal International Cyber Olympiad (ICO)	Class 1-12
2.	Eduheal International English Olympiad (IEO)	Class 1-12
3.	National Interactive Math Olympiad (NIMO)	Class 1-12
4.	National Interactive Science Olympiad (NISO)	Class 1-12
5.	International General Knowledge Olympiad (IGO)	Class 1-12
6.	National Space Science Olympiad (NSSO)	Class 1-12

Humming Bird Education		
S. No.	**Name of Exam**	**Grade**
1.	Humming Bird Commerce Competency Olympiad (HCC)	Class 1-12
2.	Humming Bird Cyber Olympiad (HCO)	Class 1-12
3.	Humming Bird English Olympiad (HEO)	Class 1-12
4.	Humming Bird General Knowledge Olympiad (HGO)	Class 1-12
5.	Humming Bird Hindi Olympiad (HHO)	Class 1-12
6.	Humming Bird Mathematics Olympiad (HMO)	Class 1-12
7.	Humming Bird Science Olympiad (HSO)	Class 1-12
8.	Humming Bird Aptitude and Reasoning Olympiad (ARO)	Class 1-12
9.	Humming Bird Spelling Competition (Spell BEE)	Class 1-12
10.	Humming Bird Language Olympiad	Class 1-12
International Assessments for Indian Schools (IAIS) (MacMillan and EEA Collaboration)		
S. No.	**Name of Exam**	**Grade**
1.	IAIS Maths Olympiad	Class 3-12
2.	IAIS ScienceOlympiad	Class 3-12
3.	IAIS English Olympiad	Class 3-12
4.	IAIS Digital Technologies Olympiad	Class 3-12
SilverZone Foundation		
S. No.	**Name of Exam**	**Grade**
1.	International Informatics Olympiad	Class 1-12
2.	International Olympiad of Mathematics	Class 1-12
3.	International Olympiad of Science	Class 1-12
Unified Council		
S. No.	**Name of Exam**	**Grade**
1.	Unified Council Cyber Exam	Class 1-12
2.	Unified International English Olympiad.	Class 1-12
3.	Unified International Mathematics Olympiad (UIMO)	Class 1-12
Unicus		
S. No.	**Name of Exam**	**Grade**
1.	Unicus Non-Routine Mathematics Olympiad (UNRMO)	Class 1-11
2.	Unicus Mathematics Olympiad (UMO)	Class 1-11

3.	Unicus Science Olympiad (USO)	Class 1-11
4.	Unicus English Olympiad (UEO)	Class 1-11
5.	Unicus Cyber Olympiad (UCO)	Class 1-11
6.	Unicus General knowledge Olympiad (UGKO)	Class 1-11
7.	Unicus Critical Thinking Olympiad (UCTO)	Class 1-11
CREST (Online Mode)		
S. No.	**Name of Exam**	**Grade**
1.	Mathematics (CMO)	Classes KG-10
2.	Science (CSO)	Classes KG-10
3.	English (CEO)	Classes KG-10
4.	Computer (CCO)	Classes 1-10
5.	Reasoning (CRO)	Classes 1-10
6.	Spell Bee Summer (CSB)	Classes 1-8
7.	Spell Bee Winter (CSBW)	Classes 1-8
8.	Mental Maths (MMO)	Classes 1-12
9.	Green Warrior Olympiad (GWO)	Classes 1-12

How To Apply?

Anyone willing to participate in the Olympiad exam can follow these steps to apply for the exam:

- Log in to the official website of the conducting organization.
- Find the Registration Option to register
- Fill up the details such as Student Name, Parent Name, School Name, Class, Postal Address, E-mail Address, Password, etc.
- Select the subjects you want to apply for. Pay the necessary registration fees and you are done.
- You will receive necessary details on your email id.

There are no minimum marks required by the Olympiad conducting organizations to apply for the exam.

Awards

Based on the organization rules, students as well as schools participating in these exams are awarded with several recognitions based on the marks they score.

⏰⏰⏰

www.ingramcontent.com/pod-product-compliance
Lightning Source LLC
Chambersburg PA
CBHW080557090426
42735CB00016B/3272